Bee Sex Essentials

Lawrence John Connor
Wicwas Press

Preface by Dr. David Tarpy, Ph.D., North Carolina State University

Featuring anatomy photos by Dr. Anita Collins, Ph.D. (retired) and Virginia Williams, USDA Bee Laboratory, Beltsville, MD

All other photos by the author unless otherwise credited.

www.wicwas.com and www.honeybeespeak.com

Published by Wicwas Press, Kalamazoo, Michigan

First edition, Second printing with corrections

Procedures and methods outlined in this book may change when used by different beekeepers operating under varied conditions and when using different genetic stocks.

Earlier versions of certain sections of this book first appeared in *Bee Culture* Magazine, Medina Ohio, Kim Flottum, editor, and *The American Bee Journal*, Joe Graham, editor.

Special thanks to Diane Rinehart for her helpful suggestions to the manuscript, and Rollie Hannan Jr., James Conklin and other beekeepers for use of their bees in taking many of the photographs included in the book.

ISBN 1-878075-22-5

Humbly dedicated to my valued teacher and queen rearing, bee breeding and instrumental insemination coach, Dr. G.H. "Bud" Cale, Jr.

Table of Contents

Preface

David Tarpy, Ph.D.,
North Carolina State University, Raleigh

Throughout history, honey bees have served as the quintessential example of chastity for poets, politicians, and religions. If they only knew . . .

Humans have been raiding honey bee colonies since before time was time (more accurately, for at least the past 10,000 years). Their bountiful harvest, their feared defensiveness, and their mysterious nature caused them to be closely associated with the afterlife, the supernatural, and the divine. Their secrecy was uncovered by Aristotle (384-322 BC), who wrote extensively on his observations of bees in the treatise *Historia Animalium*. While he accurately described many complex aspects of their biology (such as their extensive division of labor and castes), he assumed—incorrectly, of course—that the "leader" of the hive was a male or "king". Moreover, he cogently argued that bees were chaste and did not copulate, something that was a common belief at the time. The Roman poet Virgil (70-19 BC) perhaps said it best when he wrote "[Bees] indulge not in conjugal embraces, nor idly unnerve their bodies in love..." Instead, Aristotle drew upon lessons from other animal systems (such as certain fish) to argue that bees were androgynous (both male and female) and could beget offspring asexually. Not altogether untrue, given the phenomena of thylotoky and arrhenotoky, but not exactly accurate either.

The spontaneous generation of bees, and most other life forms for that matter, wasn't really questioned until the 1600s. Prior to Francesco Redi's famous 1668 experimental use of glass jars that proved fly maggots did not derive directly from raw meat, Charles Butler (1560-1647) reported his observations that honey bee "kings" lay eggs in the 1609 *Feminine Monarchie*. Perhaps it was more readily acceptable to recognize the "ruler" of a society as female following the long and successful reign of Elizabeth I, but nonetheless it was becoming clear that colonies were led by queens and that they were in fact reproductive.

Further evidence came with the advent of the microscope in the early 17th century. Specifically, the brilliant yet troubled Dutch scientist Jan Swammerdam (1637-1680) drew remarkably detailed portraits of both the queen and drone reproductive structures in his 1668 *Historia Insectum Generalis*, proving that queens were indeed females (with highly active ovaries) and drones were male (with large seminal vesicles). Even so, he still rejected the notion of copulation being required for successful reproduction—since he literally couldn't figure out how the pieces fit—but rather favored the idea that some mysterious "association" was necessary between queens and drones for fertilization to occur; he called it *aura seminalis*, where queens were impregnated by the "odoriferous effluvia" from the drones (what Swammerdam didn't realize, of course, was that a drone needs to turn his endophallus inside out in order to copulate).

It wasn't until 1821 when the blind Swiss watch-maker, François Huber (1750-1831), published his observations (through the eyes of his assistant, François Burens) that queens needed to fly from the hive in order to lay viable eggs. Queens would return with their abdomens ". . . distended by a substance, thick and hard, very much resembling the matter in the vessels of the male; completely similar to it indeed in colour and consistence," the so-called 'mating sign'. Around the same time, the German Priest Johannes Dzierzon (1811-1906) discovered and named the spermatheca, the queen's sperm storage organ. He also was the first to demonstrate male parthenogenesis (drones developing from unfertilized eggs), as well as proving that insemination was necessary for queen fecundity (through an elegant yet simple experimental design: he placed newly mated queens onto a block of ice to prevent sperm from migrating into the spermatheca).

In 1821, François Huber reported that the queen must fly from the hive to lay worker eggs.

Despite these advances, it was still assumed that queens mated only once. In the 1940s, however, USDA researchers E. Oertel and W. C. Roberts separately reported that many queens return to their hives on successive days with mating signs, demonstrating that some queens mate with at least more than one drone. In the 1960s, Norman Gary captured the copulatory act on film, showing that tethered queens mate with many drones on a given mating flight and effectively proving that queen bees were highly polyandrous.

Since then, our pursuit of "bee sex" has shifted from describing the behavior to understanding the mechanism. Specifically, there has been an increase in research on genetics and breeding. Gregor Mendel, the Austrian monk who is often recognized as the father of modern genetics, utterly failed at crossing honey bees because he didn't realize queens mated with multiple drones outside of the hive (thankfully, of course, otherwise he would have never provided such ground-breaking insights into genetics with his pea plants). In addition to his observations of mating behavior, in 1814 Huber attempted to artificially inseminate a queen with drone semen on the end of a hair-brush pencil, but to no avail. The first modern attempts at instrumental insemination were performed by USDA researchers Watson, Nolan, and Mackensen in the 1920s and 1930s, using carbon dioxide to sedate the queen, metal hooks to open her sting chamber, and a glass syringe to collect and inject semen. Harry Laidlaw perfected the process in 1944 by describing the necessity of circumventing the tissue known as the valve fold that had limited previous successes. The half century since has seen incredible advances in our understanding of honey bee genetics, from describing the Mendelian inheritance of hygienic behavior, to the mapping of quantitative trait loci, to the recent publication of the entire honey bee genetic sequence. We are therefore entering into a very exciting era of honey bee science and beekeeping, based on over two millennia of experience and with the promise of many more insights to come.

This book, *Bee Sex Essentials*, provides not only the background information necessary to understand honey bee genetics and breeding, it also contains a wealth of practical information in how to put what we know to good use. In doing so, the book calls upon every beekeeper—including YOU—to implement your own breeding program. Doing so does not require training in instrumental insemination or learning overly complicated beekeeping procedures, but simply the basic recognition of the importance of the genetic make-up of your colonies and some basic management techniques that anyone can incorporate into their operation so that they may maintain healthy genetic stock. Similar to the proliferation of microbrewers in the 1990s that transformed how we buy and drink beer, we have the opportunity to develop "microbreeders" within our beekeeping community that will enable us to control our own genetic destiny.

It took us over 2,000 years to change our view of honey bees from king-ruled cities of sexless servants to highly cooperative matrilineal kin groups. It need not take nearly as long for us to recognize the importance of honey bee genetics and the power within each beekeeper to harness it.

"Microbreeder" Rollie Hannan, Jr., of Southbury, CT checks queen cells.

Introduction

The complex biology involved in the reproductive process of honey bees continues to fascinate beekeepers and challenge researchers. These challenges have been exacerbated now that tracheal and varroa mites are found throughout North America, and African bees have expanded their range throughout the southern and western parts of the United States. All of this has challenged previously accepted standards and methods of keeping bees. As research reveals dramatic new information about the reproductive biology of the hive, beekeepers must strive to learn more about the basics of honey bee reproduction—bee sex—and how to incorporate this knowledge into their hive management plan.

My professional career had just started at The Ohio State University as Extension Entomologist in Apiculture when I was asked, in 1976, by Dr. G.H. "Bud" Cale Jr., (the developer of the Starline and Midnite hybrid bees), to establish and operate a bee breeding and instrumental insemination facility in southern Florida. My job responsibilities included the maintenance, production and distribution of the Starline and Midnite grafting stock along with the added "opportunity" of mass-producing instrumentally inseminated queen bees for production colonies used by beekeepers. This was a period of total immersion and rapid evolution of my personal knowledge of bee sex, from the mechanics of producing queens to the complexities of stimulating drone production to supply the enormous numbers of male bees required for the semen collection process that is a key part of instrumental insemination.

The program was co-sponsored and primarily financed by Dadant and Sons, Inc., of Hamilton Illinois, and by Mr. Harvey York of the York Bee Company of Jesup, Georgia. Several Starline and Midnite cooperators were also investors. Our firm, Genetic Systems, Inc., produced tens of thousands of instrumental inseminated queens each year for four years. Not all were sold. It was a tremendous undertaking, and quickly proved how little we knew about the refined aspects of quality and quantity production of drone and queen bees using instrumental insemination techniques.

The program may have been ahead of its time, and certainly the plan to mass produce thousands of instrumentally inseminated queens and sell them at a price comparable to naturally mated queens was flawed. Simply put, we did not have all the answers to key questions about bee biology regarding queen sexuality and development.

Some thirty years later, many of these same questions remain unanswered. Now beekeepers face enormous new challenges with the introduction of hive beetles, varroa and tracheal mites, and African bees. As a lecturer, author and teacher, I continue to be involved in the integration of our current knowledge about bee sex in light of the added challenges of the varroa mites and the African bees. This book cannot answer all our questions but may help focus our investigative lens onto key parts of bee sex that benefit the beekeeper. Even the general knowledge of "how do they do that" will prove useful for every beekeeper routinely seeking information about the workings of the reproduction beehive. Certain parts of this book were reworked from materials previously published in *Bee Culture* magazine and the *American Bee Journal.*

Varroa mites on developing drone.

The book's purpose

This book does not attempt to elevate the status of the drone to celebrity, but clearly attempts to balance the respective roles of queens and drones into their proper place within colony social biology. If this is achieved, beekeepers will do a better job of managing their production of *both* drones and queens.

We will look at the honey bee colony as a social unit, and see how both drones and queens in that unit are produced and regulated at the colony level during the swarming and supersedure process. Concepts of colony social physiology will reveal how the number and age distribution of drone are regulated. These concepts, clarified for me by Dr. Thomas Seeley (Cornell University), explain how the colony functions as an organism, how individual bees are subjected to one set of selection pressures while the entire colony is subject to other, very unique pressures. As future researchers examine the role of drones in the colony and measure their production and success, we will fill in our gaps of knowledge as we study and compare drones and queens, their production, mating and replacement.

This is not a book on how to propagate queens, although I consider it absolutely essential to anyone who attempts to raise queens. The ultimate book on this subject is Harry Laidlaw, Jr., and Rob Page, Jr.'s *Queen Rearing and Bee Breeding*. For those who wish to ease into the subject and are not interested in bee genetics I recommend Roger Morse's *Rearing Queen Honey Bees*.

Collaboration and recognition

Since the time when I was a little boy on my parents' farm in Michigan, I have been fascinated by new information about bees. There a local commercial beekeeper kept bees behind a windbreak in the backyard of our house, and I saw my first queen bee and drones. Since that time it would be impossible to list all those who have helped me, collaborated with me, and challenged me in my labor of learning about drones and queens, but I would be remiss if I did not recognize the contributions of Bert Martin, Bud Cale, Harvey York, Harry Laidlaw, Walter Rothenbuhler, Norm Gary, George Curtis, Steve Tabor, Clarence Collison, Dewey Caron, David Tarpy, John Harbo, Tom Rinderer, Marion Ellis, Chip Taylor, Jerry Loper, Gordon Waller, Anita Collins, Rick Helmich, Richard Adee, Clarence Wenner, Rob Page, Norm Rice, John Free, Eva Crane, Jerz Woyke and Tom Seeley. These are people who served as critical links in my education about queens and drones, or at least with how I deal with key concepts of queen and drone production and biology. There are many more not listed who helped flesh out the story, and my thanks to them is just as genuine. The former staff at Genetic Systems, Inc. owns a huge part of the successful parts of this book, for without them my efforts would have been lost. Our journey into the mass production of instrumentally inseminated queens was a blur of heat, passion, frustration and incredible excitement. Visiting scholar, commercial beekeeper and friend, Dr. John Kefuss has fussed at me for decades about writing something about the "Florida experience," and he receives credit as being one of my most loyal supporters and cheerleaders. Many commercial, sideline, and hobby beekeepers contributed to my knowledge, and I expect that relationship will continue to grow. Mr. Kim Flottum, my editor at *Bee Culture Magazine*, was instrumental in my forming books out of articles published in the Root Company's popular beekeeping magazine, starting with *Increase Essentials*.

Special thanks to David Tarpy for preparing the Preface of this book and suggestions that helped me put the polish on this book, and to Anita Collins for supplying images of drone and queen anatomy prepared by USDA technician Virginia Williams.

Finally, I commend the efforts of countless bees who labored and often gave their lives as my instructors, bringing me along a slow and cluttered path toward my knowledge of their secrets of what they do, and revealing, in a few brilliant moments, why they do these things. Once I think I am secure in some datum of knowledge, I know they will soon add a new chapter for me to learn. May it always be so.

Lawrence John Connor
New Haven, Connecticut and Kalamazoo, Michigan, 2005-2007

Sexually mature drone on a storage comb of the hive amid worker bees processing nectar and building honeycomb.

Overview

On queens and drones less seen

Many children over the age of two accurately identify a honey bee worker foraging on a flower, yet few children and seemingly fewer adults have ever seen the queen or drone honey bee. This fact does, of course, not keep them from claiming great knowledge of the world of queens and drones, from expert field identification to stories of their amazing powers and behaviors.

This apparent disconnect is due in part to the biology of the colony and in part to human mythology and folklore about bees. As a social organism engaged in food-gathering, the colony spreads itself out over a radius of several miles, but only workers routinely depart the hive to visit flowers or collect water. It should not be surprising that worker bees are frequently noticed by humans—from school children to senior citizens—whether a stinging episode has occurred or not.

Except for swarming, queens and drones leave the hive only to find each other and mate. Drones may be observed flying out of hives on their way to mating areas on most sunny afternoons. To see this, the observer need only be located near the entrance of the colony, a location relatively few non-beekeepers occupy comfortably. Queens—virgin queens specifically—fly and mate early in their adult life and that's it, they are done with sex. The queen is polygamous, mating with many drones during one or a few flights, while drones are monogamous, and not by choice. When a drone successfully mates, he's paralyzed by the mating process, his internal copulatory organs turned inside out at the moment of sexual union.

Drones ready to leave with a departing swarm. It is the only time they depart a hive except cleansing, orientation and mating flights.

Beekeepers see it a bit differently

Beekeepers appreciate the value of the queen bee due to her highly visible and extremely critical roles in the colony. She lays eggs and produces powerful pheromones. She is linked to the complex (and not fully understood) biological process colonies use to produce her replacement in the supersedure process, and in the production of new queens for issuing swarms. Most beekeepers respond to the queen with enthusiasm, respect and awe. It is she new beekeepers seek to find when they open a colony, to photograph and videotape, and express extreme regret if they fail to see her during a hive visit. I don't recall anyone expressing similar regret over a failed drone sighting.

Male bees do receive an emotional reception by beekeepers, but often a negative one, for they are too often viewed as a drain on the colony's food and labor resources and are thus considered expendable. The name *drone* carries with it cultural and religious associations that evolved over many hundreds of years of European and American history. To be called *a drone* in Western society identifies you as a social failure due to your lazy ways. Being a drone is something of tremendous shame. It casts individuals that do no work, and must be fed and cared for by society to maintain even the simplest level of life.

Drone honey bees have inherited this multi-layered human societal stereotyping because, unlike worker bees, they are in the colony for one purpose and one purpose only—to mate with any virgin queens they happen to encounter in a suitable mating area. *Sex is the work of the drone*, and if for some unforeseen reason all drones failed to perform their duties, bees would cease to exist. In this book we will explore the fascinating and complicated nature of drones and queens and their mating behavior. We will discuss the genetic basis for some of the things we see in the hive, and discuss ways beekeepers may benefit from this information.

Drone and virgin queen production

The European honey bee, *Apis mellifera*, L., evolved in Africa and migrated to Europe where it was isolated from other races of honey bees by shifting geological plates, uprising mountains, and barriers caused by numerous ice ages. All races of *Apis mellifera* are able to inter-mate, the definition of a species, but some demonstrate unique behaviors. European bees build up differently than African races, and there are differences in queen and drone production by all the different races. Yet they all interbreed, and are just one species.

The other honey bee species found in Asia and nearby regions do not interbred with *Apis mellifera.* They all swarm and produce queens and drones for the reproduction of the hive. They also produce queens and drones for queen replacement when an old queen is failing. Beekeepers must be sure they know what species and what race of honey bee the experts are discussing, for the behavioral differences between races create considerable confusion.

In this book I will discuss European races of honey bees unless another *race* is clearly identified. Until recently, only European honey bees were found in the United States[1], now an African race, *Apis mellifera scutulata,* in an amazing biological event, has migrated into the southern and western parts of the country. Sometimes a colony of these African bees is accidentally moved by beekeepers to northern regions and a great deal of excitement results. These bees are similar to European bees. They physically appear the same, but are statistically a bit smaller in size. They do not sting with a larger stinger, or employ a greater quantity or more deadly venom. When in their defensive behavior mode African bees may sting by the hundreds or thousands rather than by the dozens in European bees. This defensive behavior quickly gets our attention. Their drones and queens inter-mate with European drones and queens, creating hybrids with behaviors intermediate between the two parents.

In all the races of *Apis mellifera,* there is an amazing difference in how a colony's resources are given toward drone production when compared to queen production. Estimates of a healthy colony's drone production over a year range from 5,000 to 20,000 male bees (the lower number being the better guess for average colonies). Compare that to the average colony's virgin queen production for swarming and supersedure when only a dozen or so queen cells are produced, and only a very few are likely to emerge, mate and head a colony. If a colony produces a supersedure queen during the honey flow, the old queen is tolerated until she dies as the new queen takes over the colony. The next spring, the colony

[1]The Egyptian honey bee, *A.m.lamarkii* was introduced a long time ago, but no longer is found in the Americas.

Range of color patterns of drone honey bees produced from one queen. In part this reflects the diversity of the drones her mother mated with, since these drones have no father, but different grandfathers.

may produce two or perhaps three swarms, giving us only three or four new queens produced all season while a virtual sea of drones has been produced, flooding the brood combs, begging to be fed, eating honey and pollen, and saturating the mating areas with large numbers.

We have nothing like this dichotomy in our human experience, where the ratio of males and females is very close to 1 to 1. To us, the thousands to one imbalance of reproductive ratio found in bees is curious and seems wasteful of valuable hive resources. When we learn that most of the drones a colony produces will NEVER mate with the 3 or 4 virgins that a colony produces in a year, the imbalance seems completely out of perspective. What advantage is there for a colony to produce so many males when nearly none of them will ever mate with a queen from that same colony?

This imbalance is best explained by understanding some of the evolutionary pressures that are at work in a social unit like a bee hive. There are selection pressures on the individual drones and the individual queens found there—how healthy are they? How strong are they in flight? Are they free of disease and genetic defect? On it goes, the individual is under pressure.

Because this is a social community, the entire colony is also under selection pressure. While worker bees rarely reproduce (they do compete to lay unfertilized drone eggs if their queen fails), their most likely chance in being "winners" in the evolutionary competition is to produce strong new colonies, vigorous swarms, flooding the region with brother drones, and increasing the frequency of some of their genes in the process.

To complicate matters even more, not all the workers in the hive are genetically identical, a critical fact in colony vigor as we learn the value, the evolutionary advantage, of queens that produce colonies with worker bees with different fathers. This incredible diversity in genetic range provides bees that are better able to maintain a stable hive temperature and environment and are less likely to have disease problems because some of the drones provided genes for resistance. The number of examples of the advantage of genetic diversity continues to grow as scientists study this amazing process. I hope that human society will study and appreciate the value of genetic diversity and how it benefits the entire social community. That may be one way we will be able to reduce human conflict and work toward global peace.

When I instrumentally inseminated a virgin queen with the semen from just one drone, the queen created a colony that appeared to be normal in many ways, but the colony did not last very long, in part because the queen lacked the number of sperm she needed to produce worker offspring for several years. The other part of this was the narrowness of the colony's genetic diversity—often a technique used in many breeding programs—but robbing the colony of the genetic strength of multiple fathers and increased stability offered by a society of worker bees with different fathers.

There are undoubtedly other aspects of this male to female sexual reproductive imbalance that are important; for our purposes, we want to remember two things about it. First, it creates a numerical challenge for the beekeeper; that to obtain even a small percentage of accurate mating in nature we must saturate an area with so many drones of a desired type that extensive resources must be allocated to this function.

Second, the imbalance in production of drones and virgins helps us understanding how a single colony of bees in an isolated bee tree can produced many drones that will find unrelated virgin queens for mating. Thus each queen has the potential of producing sons that will compete with other strong and successful drones from all the colonies of the entire region. Virgins will mate with only the very strongest drones, and the resulting colony she produces will reflect not only half of her genetic material, but also the best of the drones in the *region*, providing evolutionary pressure on the individual queen, but also the collective colony. Wide-ranging genetic diversity maintains strong improvement of the *population* of colonies within the combined flight distance of both the virgin queens and the drones. This produces colonies that reflect only the most vigorous drones and virgins in the entire region. The local *Apis* gene pool is thus constantly under selection for only the most diverse population of bees. Diversity is good for honey bees.

Queen inspecting a cell prior to laying by placing her head into the cell and measuring the size of the opening with her front legs. If she inspects a drone cell, she will not release sperm and a haploid drone is produced; if she inspects a worker cell, she releases sperm so the egg is fertilized and a female bee results. Worker and queens are diploid, having two sets of

I. Drones & their development

The drone: egg laying to emergence

When worker bees provide her with clean and polished drone cells, and when stimulated by the correct conditions of nature, a queen bee will lay drone eggs in drone-sized cells. Drone brood often occupy the bottom and sides of the brood nest. Like worker eggs, queen-laid drone eggs are placed in the center of the cell bottom and are held upright by a tiny amount of cement for three days until its shell softens and it metamorphoses into a larva[2].

The total development time for drones, from egg laying to adult drone emergence, averages 24 days. There is variation in this rate. For example, larval development of drones takes between 9-10 days, compared to 7-9 days in queens or workers. The pupation time in drones runs 14-17 days, compared to 11-14 days for workers and 10-12 days for queens. The total developmental time from egg laying to emergence as an adult bee in drones is 23-27 days; in queens it is 14-17 days, and in workers it is 18-22 days. These variation are explained by seasonal conditions, variations of temperature, nutrition levels and the genetics of the bee being observed. Some races of honey bees develop more rapidly than others. The African bees in the United States have a 14-15 day queen developmental time, a day or more less than European bees developing in the same habitat. The African drone requires an average 24 days for development. This faster reproductive rate results in higher bee populations essential for survival in the tropics, and the ability to produce more swarms.

Queen's role in laying drone eggs

The queen lays drone or worker egg in response to the size of the cell. Before a queen lays an egg into either a worker or drone cell, she enters the cell with her head and upper thorax. During this inspection she must detect a chemical message informing her that

[2]The egg period for drones may extend as long as 5 days because they are on the edge of the brood nest and may experience delayed development due to non-lethal cooling. Worker bees and queens have a more stable 3-day development period during which they tolerate some variation in temperatures. In fact, under special permit, the Buckfast strain of bees has been carried from England to North America as eggs aboard airplanes. No worker bees were allowed, so it is unlikely that these eggs were kept at a constant 92-95 degree F. temperature during this interval.

Drone eggs in wax cells constructed on green plastic foundation.

the cell is clean and prepared for an egg. The queen also appears to measure the width of the cell with her fore legs. If the cell is worker-sized, she releases a small volume of spermathecal contents as the egg passes down the median oviduct. If she measures a drone cell, she does not release a volume of her spermatheca, and fertilization does not occur, resulting in a drone.

When a queen runs out of sperm, she will continue to release a volume of her spermatheca, but male bees result. The queen is called a

drone layer. Drone brood in worker cells looks like bullet shaped cells in the middle of worker brood. This happens in nature, and after single drone inseminations (SDI). At first SDI queens performed normally, but after 3-5 months of brood rearing (under Florida conditions), the sperm become depleted, but the queen continues to function as a younger, vigorous queen. Apparently lacking mechanisms to detect this change, drone-laying colonies are usually doomed.

Drone emerging from "bullet" brood.

When the queen disappears and there is no replacement in production, the worker bees lay eggs that become drones. These workers are called *laying workers*. This occurs in mating colonies or whenever the queen fails to return to the hive after her mating flight. After 28 days, a large colony will have many worker bees that have started to lay eggs. Lacking the pheromone produced by the queen that suppresses egg laying in the workers, once all brood has emerged, the workers' ovaries produce eggs. Laying workers oviposit them into worker cells—often on the sides of the cells because their abdomens are too short to reach the cell base. By definition, worker bees cannot mate and all their eggs are haploid and produce drones. There are frequently multiple eggs and larvae in the same cells as workers compete with each other. Drones that reach maturity fly out and compete with available virgin queens from other colonies. While a hopelessly queenless colony eventually dies, yet the genes from this hive—specifically from these competing workers—may enter the gene pool of neighboring hives in the form of competing drones[3].

Determination of sex in bees

The drone bees in your hive are haploid, developing without fertilization of the egg, and do not have a father. Even though no sperm merged with the queen's egg, the drone has developed with

[3]These drones are smaller, and undoubtedly are at a disadvantage in the mating area when competing with full-sized drones. While smaller drones produce viable semen, their contribution is likely a "last ditch" effort only. The production of these drones from laying workers is likely more a reflection of the queen's reproductive suppression worker bees than some sort of genetic triumph by workers.

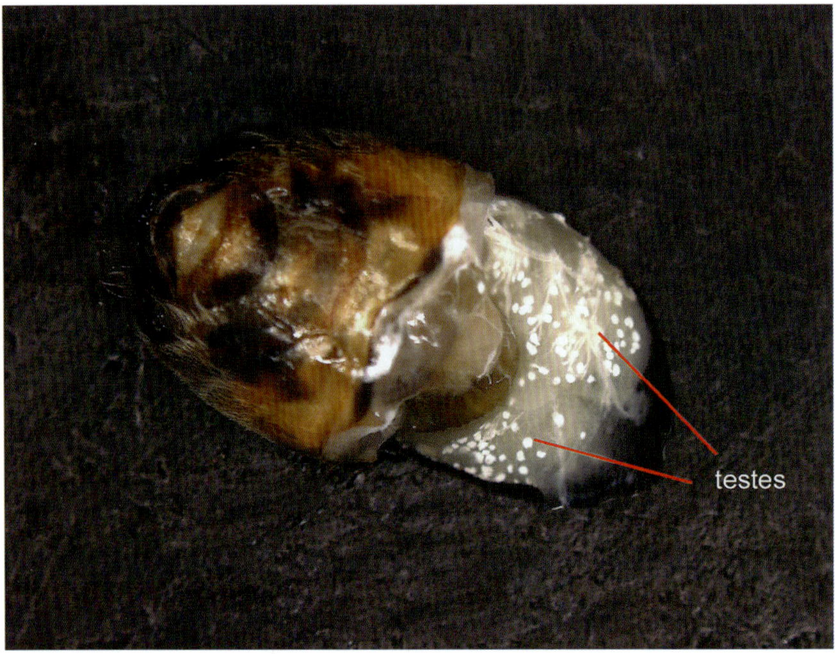

Partially dissected abdomen of a newly emerged drone, show the large paired testes, still filled with spermatazoa. The white spots are fat bodies. USDA

a single set of chromosomes.

Female bees—workers and queens—possess two sets of chromosomes, each carrying different sex determination alleles. Individual larvae with the same sex alleles are diploid male bees—diploid drones. When an egg is fertilized it has two alleles. If they are different, a female bee (worker or queen) will result. If the egg is fertilized and the sex alleles are the same, a diploid drone will result (See Section IV).

There are no diploid drones in nature. In a hive they do not live to be more than a few hours old as developing larvae, when nurse bees eat the larvae and remove all evidence of their existence. They either fail to produce normal drone pheromone or issue a *cannibalism substance*, a pheromone that worker bees recognize and respond to by eating the newly hatched diploid drone larva. When diploid drones are reared in research laboratories, they look very similar to haploid drones.

The number of sex alleles differs from bee population to bee population. If the eggs of a queen are mated to unrelated drones

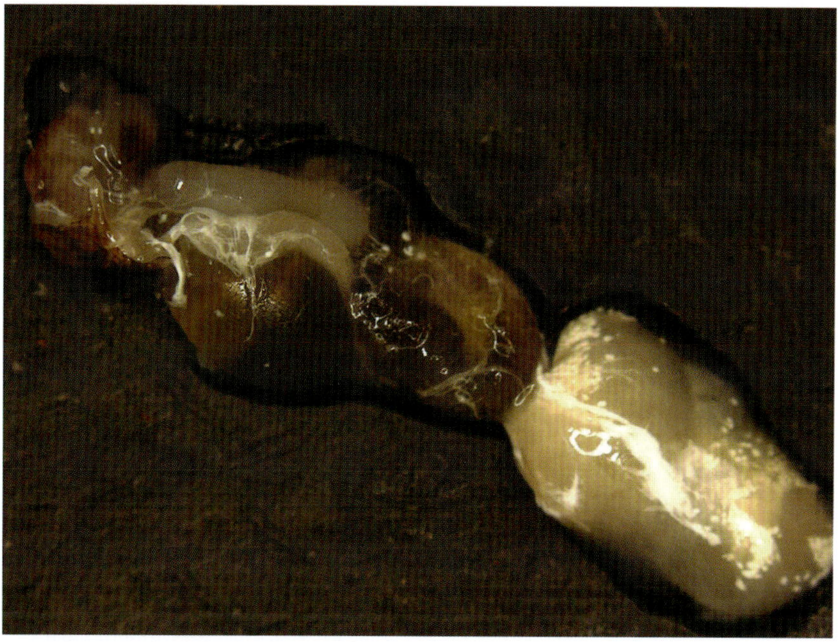

A similar shot of the abdominal contents of a young drone. Note the large testes and the full rectum. USDA

all possessing different sex alleles, all the resulting bees will be viable females. Even the best queens in the world have missing cells when the worker brood is sealed. These were eggs that were fertilized by sperm carrying the same sex determination alleles as found in the egg. Instead of developing as diploid drones, the nurse bees ate the evidence. This percentage of brood survival gives us a crude estimate of the number of sex alleles in a population. This simple chart shows you the percentage of survival of brood as determined by the number of sex alleles in a population.[4]

How many sex alleles do we have in most of our bee populations? Some estimates run as low as 11, while others run over 19—with isolation, the number is likely lower, while with extreme diversity, it is likely to be higher.

How important is the sex allele issue? In healthy, genetically diverse populations of bees, it is rarely a concern. Since queens mate with many drones, the chance of same-allele problems is reduced. Also, queens will eventually relay fresh eggs into cells

[4]Woyke, J, 1986. Sex Determination in *Bee Genetics and Breeding*, Thomas Rinderer, Editor, Academic Press, Orlando

where diploid drones were eaten, recovering part of the colony's overall productivity.

The number of sex alleles in your bees is important if you are doing any line breeding—using the best colonies from the same genetic source for queens and drones year after year—eventually *shot-gun* brood will appear. This happens in large beekeeping operations if a very small number of breeder queens are used to produce the next generation of colonies. Apparently the largest number of queens produced from one grafting mother was 50,000 daughter queens produced by a large honey production business in the Yucatan of Mexico before the area was invaded by African bees. While this is an impressive number, it sets up the potential for inbreeding and other genetic problems if a daughter queen is selected as a breeder the following season. Since the mother and daughter share sex alleles, it increases the likelihood of spotty brood when diploid drones are produced. All beekeepers, large or small, should keep a diversity of breeding stock in their breeder colonies, and these colonies should not be closely related to the previous generation of grafting mothers. Commercial beekeepers who year-after-year breed from their best queens have been shown to develop problems

This spotty brood may be due to inbreeding. It also could be a result of hygienic cell cleaning behavior. Either way, it requires a further look.

Number of sex alleles in the population	Percentage of survival of brood of a queen mated with an infinite number of drones
2	50
3	66.7
4	75
5	80
6	83.3
7	85.7
8	87.5
9	88.9
10	90
11	90.9
12	91.5

due to sex allele inbreeding when they mate queens in relatively isolated areas and never introduce new genetic materials into their breeding program.

Inbreeding was a regular concern while I ran the Genetic System bee-breeding program in Florida because we used highly inbred lines. True hybrid bees, such as the ones we produced from 1976 to 1980 under the Starline, Midnite, and Cale 876 names, required these highly inbred lines to maintain the highly desirable genetic material concentrated in them.

As in all animals, there are also recessive but lethal genes in bees that may cause the death of the developing larvae. While they are not at the same locus as used in the sex determination in bees, they are nonetheless lethal in the homozygous, highly related state.

Egg fertilization and sperm use

All bees start out as identical eggs produced by the long filaments of ovarioles that make up the two lateral ovaries in the queen bee (see photos in Section II). As the mature egg passes one of the queen's two lateral ovaries, it passes down the median oviduct. As this occurs the micropore (a small opening in the shell or chorian of the egg) aligns with the opening of a tiny tube connected to the queen's spermatheca, where potentially 5 million sperm are in storage. These sperm must successfully compete with (on average) 87 million sperm deposited into the lateral oviducts by (on average) 13 drones the queen mated with during her mating flights.

As the egg and micropore align, a small volume of the spermatheca is released, controlled by the spermathecal valve. When a queen is newly mated the concentration of sperm is high, and perhaps 50 sperm are released, all competing to fertilize the egg. In an old queen (or poorly mated queen) the number of sperm is reduced, diluted through time, so perhaps only one or two sperm are released. Once fertilized, the egg develops as a diploid individual into a worker bee unless selected to become a queen bee, when it is fed a different diet and raised in larger cells.

The queen only lays into cells that have been prepared by the bees. The bottoms of the cells are bright and shiny, and reflect light, so beekeepers say the cells have been polished. There is evidence that the bees also paint a pheromone with their tongues to attract the queen to lay into these cells; since the hive is dark, some signal is

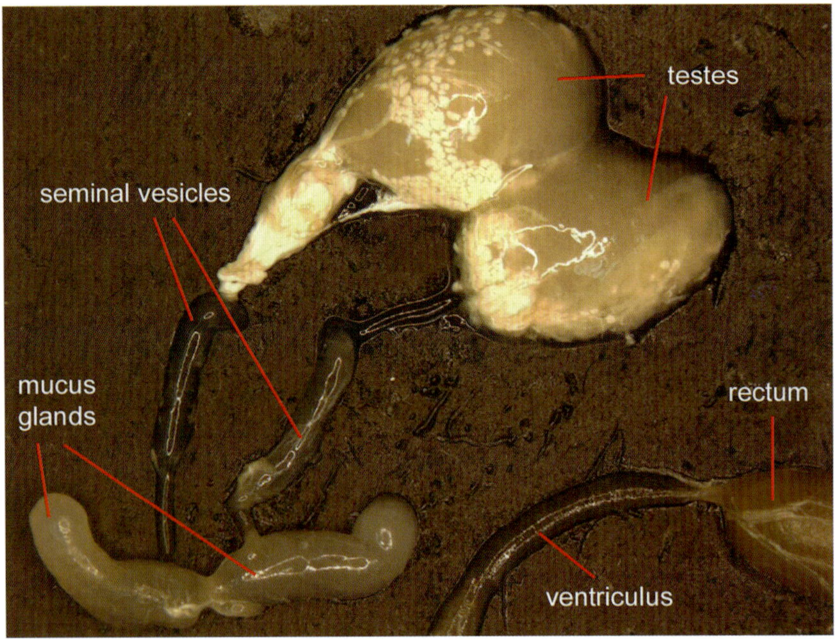

Reproductive system of a newly emerged drone. There is no mucus in the glands, and the seminal vesicles are empty and clear in color. The sperm are still in the large testes, maturing. USDA

helpful to the queen to know where to lay. Obviously a queen does not see her reflection in the polished cell bottom in the dark of the hive! A pheromonal system of stimulation for cell identification makes biological sense.

We have reviewed the key factors affecting the drone from the time of egg laying to emergence. Now we will explore drone production and population management from the colony's perspective, and introduce the concept of drone physiology.

Drone physiology

It's as if the queen and the worker bees are constantly engaged in a complicated metaphorical 'dance' within the brood nest; an elaborate and dramatic tango over the control of the production and maintenance of drones. The queen lays eggs in drone cells and the worker bees regulate their numbers, at times destroying them by cannibalizing the eggs and larvae to reduce or to eliminate them completely.

This behavioral 'dance' is performed in a series of intricate steps that reflect increasing thresholds of complexity; from its initial simple steps the dance becomes more and more complicated. It starts with the control of drone cell construction in new swarms without preexisting comb—a colony constructs drone comb at the same time it produces worker cells. It ends with the removal of the last drone after the flow is over. The dance limits or restricts the ratio, so only 17% of all cells are drone sized. In managed hives,

Worker bee dragging a returning drone from the landing area of the hive undergoing a severe drought. The time is early August in northern Ohio.

if drone comb is removed, the colony tears down worker brood and builds new drone comb. But if a colony is given only drone comb, the bees will rebuild some of the comb into worker cells. They may even raise worker bees in drone cells. The use of all plastic worker foundation causes colonies to re-engineer comb, placing drone brood perpendicular between frames or at the bottom of frames and between brood chambers.

This balancing act between the queen and the workers reflects the queen's evolutionary programming to produce as many genetic copies of her genes as possible. Drones are essentially grown-up gametes of the queen (since they do not have a father because they are haploid and

Above—Drone comb built by a new package colony, positioned at right angles between two plastic worker foundation frames. Lower left—Drone larva after sealing at lower left (with foundress varroa mite). Lower right—Pupal stage (upper bee), with purple eyes, about five days after sealing.

only have one set of chromosomes—only those of the queen). The queen's instinct seems to be to produce as many of her gametes as the colony will allow, over 5 thousand in a season in a healthy colony. While worker bees theoretically produce haploid (unfertilized) eggs, the queen's pheromones suppress ovary development in worker bees, and all the drones produced in a healthy colony are the queen's and only the queen's. If her pheromone suppression is absent, ovary development occurs in numerous workers, they will all lay eggs so that their own personal gametes may potentially fly from the hive in one last great genetic hurrah before colony death.

Meanwhile, worker bees, specifically nurse bees, follow their own genetic programming to balance the growth and maintenance of a hive so that the entire colony may reproduce by swarming. The average colony produces two or three swarms per year, so the investment in each swarm is large and represent a huge risk for both parent colony and new swarm. Nurse bees feed and groom the queen, build and maintain comb, clean cells for the queen to lay into, feed larvae as soon as they hatch, cap the cells a day or two before pupation, and clean the cells once the new adult bee has emerged. They consume pollen and nectar and secrete royal jelly, worker jelly and drone jelly—specific food mixtures for each type and age at a particular stage of development—nurse bees constantly remove food from a cell and replace it with their own.

Rich and continuous pollen reserves are required for sustained drone rearing.

If worker bees do not clean and polish the drone cells in a colony the queen will not clean them herself. She is dependant upon the workers to initiate this drone production behavior. She must be stimulated first by abundant feeding and drone cell cleaning. Several factors appear critical in triggering this response to cross the threshold into drone production.

First, there must be the right genetic programming. If you take different races of bees and manage them side by side, they will each have their own drone production cycle. We have evidence that African bees (*Apis mellifera scutelatta*) produce drones earlier and in greater numbers than do Italian bees *(Apis mellifera ligustica*). I do not have comparative data for the behavior of other stocks of great interest: Russian, Buckfast, or SMR/VSH or hygienic stocks.

Second, the time of the season must be right. Bees are enormously sensitive to changes in photoperiod, the light/dark cycle in their year. They slow all brood rearing in the fall and will eventually stop in many temperate areas but will continue to produce a small amount of brood in subtropical regions like south Florida. Experiments with photoperiod have given researchers northern drone production during midwinter in snow covered colonies. It appears that the bees are very responsive to the increasing day length and adjust their brood production accordingly. As one travels north toward the North Pole, the rate of brood rearing increases because the rate of change is greatest, and the days are longer and there are more hours for the bees to collect pollen and nectar in the northern tier of states, Canada and Alaska.

Third, bees are constantly aware of their colony's food reserves, of the amount of both pollen and stored nectar in the hive, as well as the volume of open comb for additional food storage (an empty comb ordor, established by Tom Rinderer). If there is little food in a hive, the threshold allowing drone production is not reached until abundant food is both present in the hive and coming through the entrance. In Florida I quickly learned that feeding a colony was not the only factor necessary for drone production. Each colony needed to have 20 or more pounds of stored honey, three deep frames, and some stored pollen before it became a stable drone-producing hive.

Finally, bees are very sensitive to the weather changes that interrupt incoming nectar and pollen. After a cold front many drone eggs and young larvae disappear, consumed by hungry sisters as they trim drone production due to reduced protein income.

We will now attempt to decode some of these complexities by looking at the physiology of drone production and maintenance.

Decoding drone physiology

The word physiology (in Greek *physis* = nature and *logos* = word) refers to the study of the mechanical, physical, and biochemical functions of living organisms. As a topic, physiology is left out of many beekeeping books. The listing of "physiology" under "drone" in an index is a very rare event. Authors seem to imply that physiol-

Workers building drone comb. Factors that stimulate drone cell production and drone brood rearing are part of drone physiology.

Drone brood at the bottom of the worker brood in a colony in the spring.

ogy is included under anatomy (mechanical), morphology (physical) and metamorphosis (biochemical) functions of their work. In other words, they imply that a study of drone form and function will cover the physiological aspects of drone production.

The traditional of drone development was that drones are produced as the colony grows in the spring and are expelled at the end of the nectar flow. Now we need to know so much more about the colony's *social physiology* and how it determines drone production and elimination. Social physiology asks a lot of questions. What *triggers* drone production? What *regulates* drone numbers? What *conditions* are present and mechanism(s) are used when colonies trim (eat) drone numbers? What *regulates* expulsion of older drones yet favors younger drones? (How do bees detect age in a drone?). What chemical(s) make(s) up drone pheromone, where is it produced and how does it work? (We know older open drone brood cells produce an odor very attractive to female varroa mites, biological evidence that some odor is present).

How do colonies *tolerate* drones from a drone layer or laying workers under conditions drones ordinarily would never be allowed in a colony? Is it the absence of worker brood pheromone or another trigger? What overriding control does the queen have to do with drone production? What *selection pressures* should beekeepers keep in mind when dealing with drone production and maintenance in a colony?

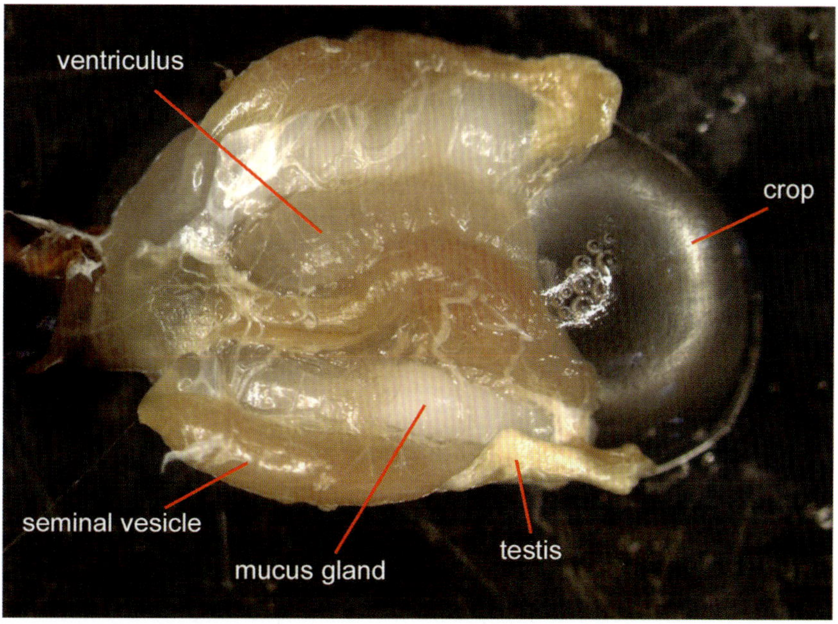

With the outer cuticle removed, you can see the digestive and reproductive systems folded up together to fit into the abdomen. USDA

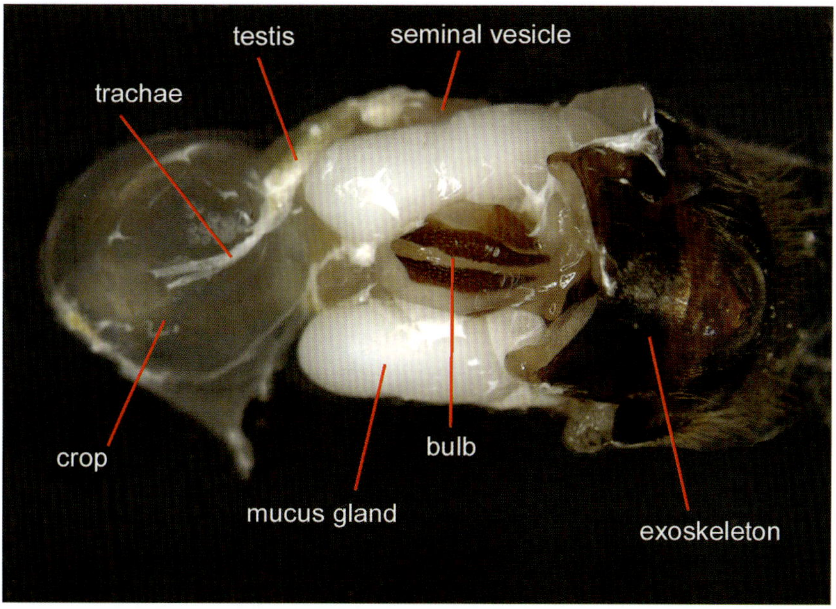

This is a view of the abdominal contents from the other side. Some of the cuticle (exoskeleton) has been left in place at the tip of the abdomen. The bulb of the penis can be seen nestled between the full mucus glands. This is a mature drone, so the testis are very small. USDA

We do not know the answer to many of these questions. Or "we don't know enough to be certain." So consider this a work in progress, one that requires us to update our knowledge about the amazing process that colonies use to produce, maintain and eliminate drones.

The queen's role in drone production

The queen bee is responsible for laying most of the eggs that become drones in a normal colony. Scientific estimates of the number of drones laid by worker bees in queen right colonies generated such a low number that the result was considered statistically zero. This changes if the queen never mates, or depletes her supply of sperm in her spermatheca. Then a young, healthy queen produces drones. The selection pressure here is clear—the queen's genes are being passed on to the pool of drones in the area even though the queen and her colony are apparently doomed.

Virgin queens produced—by the colony or by beekeepers—very early or very late in the season, or during periods of intense nectar dearth, often fail to find drones for mating. They may not be in the area because the colonies have not had conditions favoring their development. Or during the time period the virgin should mate, she may not have been able to fly to the drone congregation areas, and after several weeks produces unfertilized eggs—drone eggs[5].

At times healthy queens mate with drones, run out of sperm, and become drone layers. Research has shown that virgin queens will mate with 7 to 45 drones, with an average around 13 drones. In nature, immediately after the mating flight a queen returns to the hive holding 87 million sperm in her lateral oviducts. The queen moves muscles in her body to facilitate sperm migration into the spermatheca, while worker bees groom and touch her in such a way as to facilitate migration. Excess sperm are expelled in thin threads of material removed by worker bees.

IF drones are scarce OR the drones in an area have low sperm counts THEN there will be a reduced number of sperm in the queen's spermatheca. This has been shown to be a result of expo-

[5]If one takes a drone-laying queen out of a colony and instrumentally inseminate her months after she has started to lay unfertilized eggs, she will produce female offspring. While drone layers do not naturally mate once they begin laying eggs the sperm migration mechanism remains intact. This permits breeders to cross a queen with her son, a rapid inbreeding method.

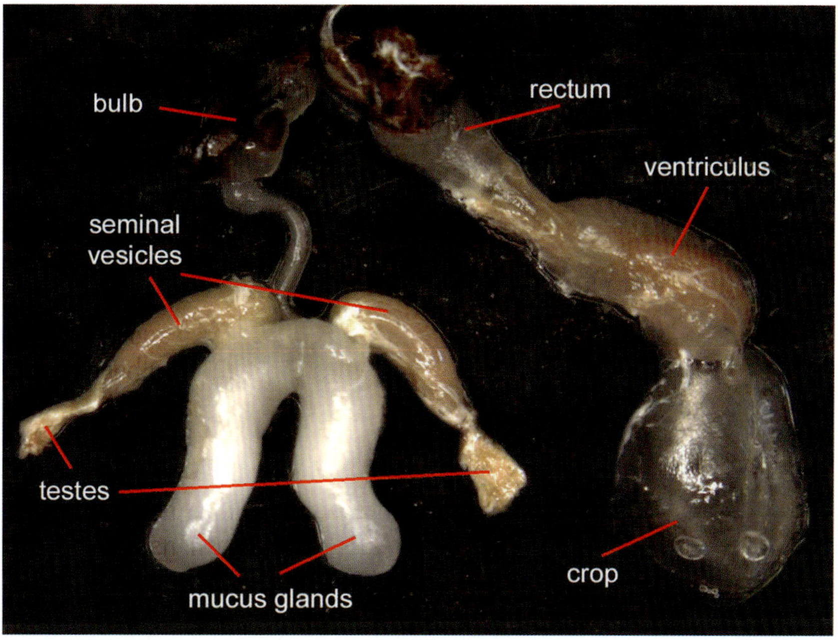

Mature, sexually active drone: The digestive system (right: crop, ventriculus and rectum) has been spread out separately from the reproductive system. The white mucus glands are very distinct from the tan seminal vesicles filled with semen. USDA

sure to certain hive chemicals, especially coumophos, used to kill varroa mites. Also, the combs in these colonies may carry enough chemical residues to functionally reduce or end sperm production in drones. Chemically exposed drones may appear healthy but be sterile, or have low sperm counts.

Nature also creates conditions when sperm counts are low. Early season drones used in mating areas of southern/western queen producers may experience cold weather that interferes with normal sperm development (as larvae) and sperm migration (as adults). Workers are apparently unable to detect drones with low sperm counts, and no selection occurs at this level.

A personal observation of this took place in several southern states, when a cold blast from the north affected drones in production in February. The queens that mated with these drones headed normal colonies for a full season, but became drone layers over the following winter, and beekeepers were startled in their first seasonal inspection to find colonies filled with drones and drone

Drones returning from a mating flight encounter a queen excluder placed in front of the hive to monitor drone flight activity.

brood. While the beekeepers were casting about like landed fish, eagerly affixing blame on the genetic stock of the bees, or perhaps some evil virus, a check of each queens' spermatheca revealed that they were nearly clear and devoid of sperm. The cause of all of this was the weather, and how it impacted a human schedule. No genetic defect or virus was involved.

The balancing act—Regulating drone numbers

Several factors have been linked to drone production in European honey bee colonies:

Increasing photoperiod—It has been shown that it is easier to stimulate drone production during increasing day length, artificially, even in the middle of winter. In south Florida it was much more difficult to produce drones after mid-October on even if the bees were in good late fall nectar flows.

Nutritional conditions—Colonies with stored pollen and nectar and colonies with stored food resources and incoming spring forage will produce drones in great numbers compared to colonies with limited food reserves which produce few or no drones. A colony with pollen in many frames in the fall that is then fed heavily will cover that pollen with stored carbohydrate. As the brood nest expands the bees will have both pollen and carbohydrate needed for worker brood production. Young nurse bees emerge and become the workers involved in the heavy production of drone brood, although all bees producing brood food are clearly involved.

Queen age—It is my observation that spring queens, new queens and older failing queens produce the greatest number of drones. When a new queen is installed in a colony, either by supersedure or by the beekeeper, there is often an increase in drone production. There are two possible explanations for this. First, there may be some selection pressure for a queen to establish a population of her genetic offspring as soon as possible. Since supersedure and queen replacements by beekeepers are usually done in good forage conditions, this is not a stress on a colony. Looking at individual colony records it was evident that as queens begin to fail—something we cannot visually see in the queen or her brood—there is a spike in drone production. This does not have anything to do with the queen being a drone layer. It indicates the colony is reacting to reduced queen pheromone or some other trigger and, if overall seasonal conditions allow, the bees foster drone production. Once an increased cycle of drones is in production, the old queen disappears and a replacement queen appears.

Worker bees feeding on disturbed drone brood positioned between frames and broken apart during colony inspection.

Because we know that bees have elaborate mechanisms to prevent inbreeding between virgin queens and drones from the same colony, the above observation has always struck me as somewhat ironic. Is this a last-ditch effort to guarantee full mating even if it means that inbreeding will take place? Or is this an expression of some selection pressure to push out a particular set of genes before the queen departs?

Measuring sealed drone cells (in square inches or number of cells) in a colony is one way to show these behaviors. If done on a 14 day interval, it will show the relative change in drone production at the same stage of development.

Brood trimming (Cannibalism)—Bees routinely trim brood as nutritional and temperature changes occur during the season. They start with drone eggs and work up the brood cycle, and will even pull out young pupae. The bees cannibalize these drones, removing whatever fluids for proteins and other nutrients.

The regulators for these behaviors are largely unknown. How does a worker bee know to eat one larva when other workers are feeding others on the same comb? Do bees measure the quality (food value) of the royal jelly and brood food given to a bee and trim those bees receiving inadequate nutrition? This would insure that only fully functional bees are produced by the colony. A key feature to the social physiology of a hive is that all individual members be useful, productive and "functional."

Drone production under 'sparse' conditions

It is useful to review one Cornell study[6] looking at drone production under good and poor forage conditions. In the study, uniform colonies were moved in June from the forage-rich areas around Ithaca, New York to a research facility in the Adirondack State Park, where bee forage is 'sparse.' The unfed group of colonies lost weight in the new location, and had significantly less drone brood in production. A group of colonies fed sugar syrup did a better job of maintaining both colony weight and drone comb

Flight departures—Soon after the colonies were moved into the new location, they were observed for drone flight. The fed colonies produced significantly more drone flight (11.1 ± 2.1 departing drones per minute) than the unfed colonies (4.7 ± 2.4 drones per minute). There had been no time for new drones to emerge and mature, so these were all drones produced under Ithaca conditions. No observations were reported on the rate of movement of drones between colonies and how this influenced these results.

Breaks in drone production—I have noticed during mid-July hive

[6]T.D. Seeley and A.S. Mikheyev. 2003. Reproductive decisions by honey bee colonies: turning investment in male production in relation to success in energy acquisition. *Insectes Soc.* 50: 134-138

Worker (left) and drone (right) self-feeding on honey in storage cells. Only very young drones require feeding by nurse bees.

inspections in Connecticut, that there were no drones in production (eggs, larvae or pupae) and relatively few drones in the colony (less than 100). The colonies appear to have had a very good nectar flow earlier in the summer but these conditions were not present at my inspection. There were many frames of pollen stored, fresh pollen in the brood nest, and plenty of eggs. Was the queen restarting brood rearing after a bit of a break? Had the colonies swarmed and the new queen was just taking over?

Drone elimination–The Cornell study looked at the number of dead adult and pupal drones in dead bee traps, but the results were affected by the growing difference in the numbers of surviving drones in each colony. It appears drones are not allowed back into the hive, as one finds a mass of drones at the bottom of the bottom board of a colony when drone rejection is underway. Worker bees may accidentally sting drones during the rejection process.

The Cornell study makes it clear that we are just starting to decode the social physiology of the drone honey bee and its production, maintenance and mating behavior as based on colony energy (carbohydrate) needs. This paper did not concern itself with protein needs. All this leads to even more questions, which the authors stated with eloquence:

"How exactly does a colony adjust its production of drones? Does the queen lay fewer unfertilized eggs when workers have less success at nectar foraging? If so, then how does the queen acquire information about the colony's success in nectar foraging? Or does the queen lay the same number of unfertilized eggs regardless of the worker's foraging success, but the workers provide less care for immature drones when the nectar foraging is poor? If so, then how do the nurse bees acquire information about the colony's success in nectar foraging? And how exactly does a colony adjust maintenance of drones? Do the workers simply withhold food from the drones when the nectar foraging deteriorates, or do they also attack the drones? Answers to all these questions must await further study."

The life of adult drones

Newly emerged or callow drones remain within the brood nest for up to 6 days where they are fed by worker nurse bees, receiving secretions of the worker hypophrangeal glands plus pollen and nectar/honey just like callow workers. At this age they stop nurse bees and beg to receive food. As they grow older the worker bees are less likely to feed them, and the drones feed themselves honey and pollen. Their lives move along a progression starting as soft bodied young drones found within the brood nest. After their bodies harden they are found on the periphery of the brood nest on the combs containing pollen and honey. They will be found there four to twelve days after emergence. These drones need the nutrition and energy of these foods to complete their sexual development. They can be seen putting their heads into pollen and nectar cells to obtain protein and carbohydrates. Finally, the sexually mature drones are found on the honeycombs, either on the outside frames in the brood chamber, or in the supers. After they make their afternoon mating flights they return to the honey cells to refuel for the next flight or to rest for the next day.

During hive inspections made during the morning when drones are not flying you can make an assessment of the age of drones by testing the hardness of their bodies and watching their movement on the combs. Very young drones are impassive when you press a finger against their thorax. Their bodies are still relatively soft, and their abdomens are filled with light colored and strong smelling fecal material since they have not taken a cleansing/orientation flight. Drones that are older will have a more solid thorax and their rectums are filled with darker fecal materials, and will actively move away if touched on the thorax. Finally, the sexually active drones will often fly away, and become very active when they are touched. Their rectal contents are mostly clear, often floral scented, and indicate a diet of primarily carbohydrates. In the afternoon we observe the drones flying in and out of the hive. By marking drones at one hive, you can record their flight times as well as observe their drifting from hive to hive in the apiary.

Drones have not been observed feeding other bees, but may serve to take excess nectar during a strong flow period. Orientation/cleansing flights start anywhere from six to nine days after emergence but drones may delay mating flights anywhere from 12 to 18 days, depending on local conditions and the strain of bees. The initial mating attempts of drones average 30 minutes. As drones reach 31-40 days of age, they will take longer mating flights, the longest recorded being over 200 minutes. Males will make multiple mating attempts during the same afternoon. Since the drones are constantly in flight during the mating attempt, they must consume considerable amounts of honey; this may explain why beekeepers find exhausted drones on the ground or on vegetation. There is no evidence of drone foraging as occurs in other bee species.

Mating flights vary by geographic location, and from early spring to mid summer to fall, apparently adjusting for day length and flight conditions. Bee race influences drone flight time. This is of particular interest with African bees where African drones are more likely to be flying when European and African virgins are flying, while European drones fly only during the flight time of European virgins. Some time between one and four in the afternoon you can observe drones leaving the colony and making mating flights. Don't be confused with cleansing/orientation flights young drones make during the same time period. Like orientation flights of worker bees, the inexperienced drones fly in front of the hive in circles of increasing radius. If drones are confined to the hive for several days due to high winds or poor weather, the next favorable mating flights will start earlier. During extremely hot days flight time may be delayed to when temperatures are cooler.

Drone longevity is correlated with the quantity and quality of pollen feeding in the late larval period and the early adult life prior to mating flights. The duration of the mating flights appears to be related to feeding prior to departure.

Bee colonies in apiaries reflect the remarkable drifting behavior of drones when they return to the apiary. Perhaps drones are less precise in their orientation, but there appears to be another behavior at work. Drones constantly move to new colonies in the apiary and eventually even adjoining apiaries as they seek out those colonies that are taking exceptional care of drones: colonies under going queen replacement. During September and October hive inspections it is not unusual to find small queen right colonies without any male bees in the colony; none at all can be found. Stronger colonies may have some adult drones on the pollen and nectar frames, but no drones in development, or at the last stage of pupal development. In colonies of any strength that are undergoing queen replacement, either in the emergency, swarming or supersedure mode, you usually find drones. We created colonies with a caged virgin as a favorable environment to house and feed drones when other colonies were unwilling to do so.

The movement of drones from hive to hive and even apiary to apiary is remarkable. I have observed drones that drifted to queenless colonies at the start of nectar dearth from a distance of five or six miles. This means that at less favorable times of the year the drones in your hives have accumulated from colonies in a radius of five to ten miles. This is a huge frustration to the beekeeper who intends to produce queens mated to a desired drone stock. We will discuss (Section III) the combined movement of drones and virgin queens as a mechanism of increasing mating to unrelated, yet highly vigorous stock. Drone drifting has been shown to be a key mechanism in the transmission of both the tracheal and varroa mites, both of which are carried to the field by drones and then to new hives as the drones move about. Finally, drones and virgin queens mate in both drone congregation areas and in bee flyways.

Drones and the honey crop

Traditionally drones are either ignored by beekeepers, or considered some sort of enemy because they consume the honey crop. Historically, most beekeepers don't think much about drones, and rarely have. For example, in Dr. C. C. Miller's *Fifty Years Among the Bees*, drones are listed in the Index only once, that being "Drone-laying queens". By comparison, there were three-dozen references to "Queens".

Drones have been seen, and continue to be seen by some beekeepers, as a drain on a colony's honey production. Granted, if a colony produces between five and twenty thousand drones over the course of a season, this is a considerable investment in hive resources. Yet the presence of drones may actually have some possible positive effects on the hive. Even the drone's long periods of inactivity within the hive may be important to sperm maturation and migration, so that a quiet drone is actually working, but passively—if the drone's business is sex with the queen, anything that helps the drone perform this task is to the colony's ultimate advantage.

Mature drone, partially everted—abdomen and thorax muscles harden. USDA

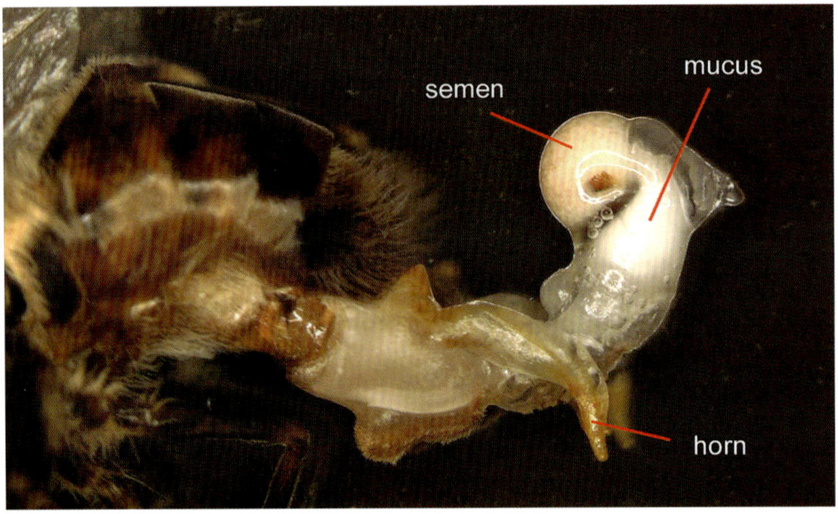

Complete eversion of endophallus (penis) of the drone, showing the tan semen and the white mucus.

Colonies only produce drones when foraging conditions justify an expenditure of resources on this investment, and when started, only in the numbers the colony is able to support. Efforts to reduce drone production in healthy colonies by removing drone combs inevitably results in the colony being forced to rebuild worker combs into drone sized cells. Drones may actually reduce some of the pressure of retuning foragers during a nectar flow. We know that foragers do not process nectar themselves, but must find a house bee to take the nectar and start the ripening process. In colonies with large drone populations, the house bees are being relieved of nectar by begging drones, thus freeing the house bees to take the nectar of a newly returned forager.

Finally, the location of drone brood in the hive and the larger cell and adult body size of drones suggest that the drones themselves may contribute to temperature regulation and cluster temperature stability. With drone brood located predominately at the bottom and edge of the brood nest, and since heat rises, it will serve as a source of warmth for the bees on cold days. Should the cold spell be severe, the drones may die in the brood nest, while thermally protecting developing worker brood and queen cells from the same fate. No research has confirmed this role.

One other unique view of drones was presented by Connecticut commercial beekeeper/queen breeder, Allan Latham. In his book[7] Latham wrote about the importance of the drones as a stimulus to worker bees. While I agree that the drones are undoubtedly a stimulus in the hive, I am sure that Latham is wrong in saying that the stimulus is sexual in nature, since there has never been any evidence of any sexual activity between worker bees and drones.

My own theory—and it may be incorrect—is that worker-bees in colonies blessed with numerous drones labor more eagerly than those having few drones. Is it not possible that the mere presence of drones stimulates the workers to greater activity? Everyone knows that young women spending summer weeks at the seashore find it boring if no men are present. Although the worker-bee is an imperfect female, this fact does not preclude the possibility that she may be stimulated by the presence of the male. At any rate, I have never seen a smaller surplus stored in a hive with many drones than in a hive with few drones. The amount of surplus in a hive is determined by the activity of the working force, and I have always noticed that where drones are numerous, the bees were very active.

Overlooking his sexual anthropomorphisms, Latham's observations on the stimulative value of drones are valid, and one we need to remember. Rather the sexual component Latham describes, it's likely that drones stimulate worker bees by their food begging and other unknown behaviors. His end conclusion is correct, it is the vigorous field force of bees in a strong colony that can produce and maintain drones that will produce the largest honey crop. Inevitably, honey production comes down to the number of bees that can leave the hive and collect a nectar crop when it becomes available. We find that the strongest hives produce the most honey, and the strongest hives produce the most drones.

When asked, commercial beekeepers are hard pressed to show me a healthy, queen-right colony that contains too many drones. In my Florida life I needed unrelated drones to use for insemination for drone mothers (since the males a queen produces are not genetically related to the drones she mated with, any unrelated, random drones worked fine). I put out a plea to beekeepers to shake packages of bees from the outside frames of the hive where

[7]Allen Latham, *Allen Latham's Bee Book.* 1949. Hale Publishing Company, Hapeville, Georgia. Page 52

drones reside on the pollen and nectar cells. When shaken into a package cage with queen excluder material on the sides, workers were smoked out to safely use the drones in the lab.

When offered cash for drones, several beekeepers went out one fine fall Florida day to bring back boxes of drones. Instead they returned with a scant dozen drones in the cage. The bee colonies clearly did not contain as many drones as the beekeeper thought. If a colony produces 5,000 drones over the entire season, and the drone-producing season is from April to September, then there are about 25 weeks that drones are in development. On a weekly basis only 200 drones (5,000÷25) are being added to the colony. If drones live two months in the hive from egg to death (an optimistic view), then there would be about 1,600 drones at any one time in *all* stages of development, about half of which would be adults and only a quarter of them actually making mating flights. It is a tight ship the bees run, and they keep the drones at a frugal yet optimal level during the season.

Drone availability in an "average" colony throughout the season at the 40-45th parallel, emerging 5000 drones total for the year, half of which reach sexual maturity and are able to mate with virgins. This colony does not have a summer of fall nectar flow. Drone production is not equal throughout the season but depends on natural bee cycles of colony buildup, swarming behavior and the availability of food and water. Based on the author's experience.

Month	Monthly drone production, at emergence	Number of drones reaching sexual maturity	Maximum number of virgins mated at 20 drones per queen
April	1200	200	10
May	1500	700	35
June	1200	840	42
July	800	420	21
August	200	200	10
September	100	120	6
October	0	20	1

In Florida the drone production season took place in two parts. Drones were produced from late January to May, when a dearth eliminated them until the late summer/fall flow from Brazilian pepper stimulated a second surge of drone production. Drone production was usually over by mid October, but adult drones could last in certain colonies for weeks and in mild winters, over the winter. A cold front often ended their lives.

We must remember that drones are part of a normal, healthy, disease and mite free colony. Because colonies support drones only when seasonal and forage conditions dictate, they freely invest in drone production only when their incoming pollen and nectar "assets" are in abundance. Likewise, when the season is finished, drones are prevented from returning to hives after making mating flights. They often flock together under the entrance of the hive, or are drawn into a colony that is undergoing late season swarming or queen replacement. The drones will be cared for until the queen starts to lay eggs. Then these drones will disappear as well. A colony that contains drones during the winter indicates a poor queen and certain problems ahead.

One method beekeepers are able to use to prolong the drone season is to establish one hive as a queenless unit until all possible mating is completed; this hive may then be combined with another. Finally, the absence of drones in a colony when others have drones should prompt the beekeeper to ask the question *why are there*

Worker bee and chalkbrood mummified drone pupa. Drone brood is very susceptible to the fungal disease unless selected for resistance.

no drones? This can be on additional tool used to evaluate stock, colony development and overall acceptability.

Quote without comment:

"Males, known as drones, perform no useful function except to mate. They are loutish and filthy . . ."[8]

Queen cells at the top of a brood comb. The second cell from the left is the most mature, as evidenced by the removal of the wax.

[8]Elizabeth Kolbert, "Stung, Where have all the bees gone?" *The New Yorker,* August 6, 2007.

II. Queens and their development

Queen development

During supersedure and emergency queen replacement worker bees decide which newly hatched worker larvae will have their cells modified and diet changed to become queen larvae. There is contradictory evidence to suggest that there is competition between workers with different drone fathers (see Subfamilies and Super-sisters) to select full sister larvae with the same drone father to become queens and preventing sisters with different drone fathers from reaching queen status. During swarming the old queen lays into the queen cups workers have prepared for her by cleaning and adding new wax and thinning the perimeter of the cup. In swarming, the queen determines the initial pool of future queen candidates but not the timing of their production. This does not prevent the worker bees acting as genetically controlled political strategists that impact final queen selection.

Since queens develop from fertilized eggs developmentally identical to the worker eggs, worker and queen eggs hatch at the same time when kept under the same conditions, in about three days. For five additional days the queen larvae are fed food produced by the worker bees called *royal jelly*; a special food that they feed all young bees, but especially developing queen larvae from the time of selection as a future queen to the time the queen cell is sealed. Ordinarily worker bees produce royal jelly in surplus for the last-stage larva, and residual royal jelly should be found in a well-reared queen cell once the queen has emerged. The cell is sealed by the workers and then the queen larva spins a cocoon inside the cell and undergoes her complex metamorphosis

Female larva about 12 hours after hatching on a grafting tool. This the ideal age used to produce queens in rearing operations when abundant royal jelly facilitates transfer.

from larvae to pupa to adult. The virgin queen emerges from the cell 6.5 to 7 days later as a fully developed virgin queen, taking between 14 to 16 days for total development.

When sexually mature the queen leaves the colony to mate with drones. This is usually ten to twelve days after she emerged from the cell, but may be as little as 6-7 days (some say less) or as long as 18 days. She first makes orientation and cleansing flights a few days after emergence—not to be confused with mating flights.

During mating a virgin queen receives 87 to 200 million sperm from an average of 13 drones. The seminal fluids are temporarily stored in her bursa copulatrix and the median and lateral oviducts. She makes one or more mating flight to obtain this number of sperm, mating with as many as 45 drones (average is 13) to obtain this supply. Each drone may produce as much as one microliter of seminal fluid containing, on average, 5 million spermatozoa. Since the queen's median and lateral oviducts are filled with sperm when she returns to the hive she uses the muscles of her body and the grooming and massaging by worker bees to stimulate sperm migration into the sperm storage structure in her body, called the *spermatheca*. Surplus fluids are expelled from her vagina as thin

Newly emerged cell (partially damaged by the beekeeper). Without egg production her body is still small; she moves quickly around the hive.

Rapidly expanding colony in early spring. This queen is being fed so well she is depositing two eggs in some cells. As the colony expands, the bees will keep up by cleaning more brood cells and duplicate eggs should disappear.

threads of seminal materials and carried off by the worker bees.

Out of all these sperm only 4 to 8 million sperm enter the spermatheca. While this seems to be highly inefficient, it may be compared to the intense sperm competition seen throughout the animal kingdom. If sperm do not migrate (or are not purged) from her body within 48 hours there may be a mass of solidified sperm blocking the passage of eggs down the median oviduct. This may cause the death of the queen or abnormal laying behavior.

Inside the queen's abdomen is a pair of ovaries holding up to 370 ovarioles or egg tubules that are joined to one of two lateral oviducts. This leads to the median oviduct that is part of the vaginal orifice; this enlarges to form a vaginal chamber that has a finger-like ribbed structure called the vaginal *valvefold*. The valvefold muscles open and close passage to the oviduct. This valvefold makes instrumental insemination a challenge, since it must be moved out of the way in order for the syringe to enter the median oviduct, and allow the sperm to emter her body. The average spermatheca holds about one microliter of fluid, and is connected to the oviduct by the spermathecal duct. This duct has muscles attached to it that pump the sperm—into the spermatheca after mating—and out again during sperm release during egg laying.

A large, dark queen. Three abdominal segments extend past her wings.

Queen size

Since the spermatheca is a sphere, any technique that increases the size of the queen, and thus the size of the spermatheca, allows the queen to carry many more sperm. My cousin, Jim Conor, calculated that a ten percent increase in the diameter of the spermatheca results in a 24 percent increase in the volume for potential sperm storage. This could mean that a queen with 24% more sperm might lay eggs for a year or more longer than a smaller queen[9].While it may be extraordinarily difficult to increase the size of full-realized, optimum queens, it shows the inherent danger of producing small queens under poor queen rearing conditions. In addition to a smaller spermatheca, smaller queens have fewer ovarioles and a lower egg-laying rate. Absolutely anything that interferes with the development of the queen and her eventual size will interfere with the performance of the queen, the number of her ovarioles, and the size of her spermatheca.

Egg laying by the queen bee

The number of eggs a queen lays each day is difficult to quantify. However, we can estimate egg laying indirectly by measuring the amount of brood, usually sealed, produced within a brood cycle. If we look at the peak brood rearing period starting in late winter and continuing to late spring—a four or five month interval—we find that productive queens lays between 1,200 and 1,800 eggs per day, as based on the amount of brood present in a colony, and adjusted for missing diploid drones, chilled brood and brood eaten by workers. As the brood season starts, the daily rate is slower,

[9]Jim Conor, Allegan, Mich., Personal communication. (Jim is my uncle's grandson. There are five variations among five brother uncles on the spelling of the family name—I like the version that it was a way to circumvent anti-nepotism laws in effect during the Great Depression. Several or all of the brothers worked for the same factory at one time or another.)

but it increases dramatically with warmer nighttime temperatures and fresh food supplies to the hive. If nights are frigid or food reserves are limited (as during poor weather), the egg-laying rate will drop.

If a single queen lays 1,500 eggs per day for 20 days—the interval needed for worker bee development—we can predict the number of expected brood frames in the hive. A square inch of worker brood cells produces about 25 cells, so this queen lays about 60 square inches of worker brood each day:

$$\frac{\text{Number of cells laid per day}}{\text{Number of cells per square inch}} = \frac{1{,}500}{25} = 60\ \text{in}^2/\text{day}$$

To compute the amount of brood produced in an early summer brood rearing period, we simply multiply 60 in^2/day by 20 days, the fastest development rate of European stock worker bees, and get 1,200 in^2 of brood in a colony. Since a standard deep Langstroth frame measures roughly 17 x 9 inches, it holds about 150 square inches of brood *per side*, or about 300 square inches *per frame*. When we divide 1200 square inches of brood by 300 inches per frame, we see that this queen produces four *completely full* frames of brood in a 20 day period.

Since it is rare to find brood frames where every cell in a comb is filled with brood, a normal colony with 1200 square inches of brood has it spread out over six to ten frames. If the bees leave a two-inch border around the brood area, it reduces the brood to 13 x 5 inches, or 65 inches/

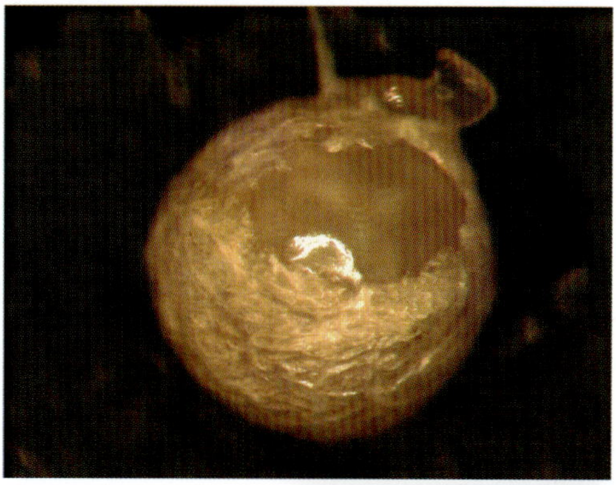

Above: Spermatheca from a mated queen, with the covering of trachea partially removed to reveal the tan seminal fluids inside. Below: Virgin queen's spermatheca is water clear. USDA

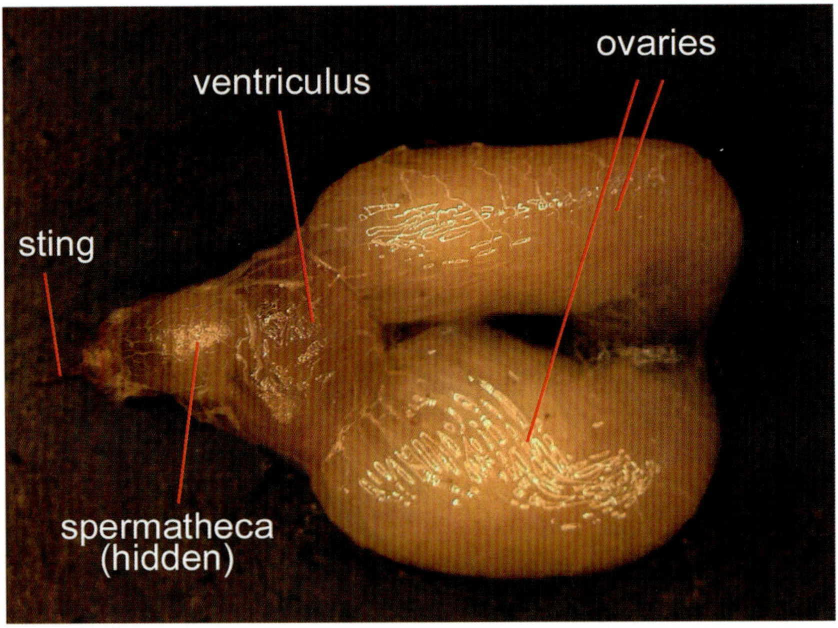

Inside the abdomen of a laying queen. It shows the large ovaries, the digestive tract and the sperm storage organ, the spermatheca.

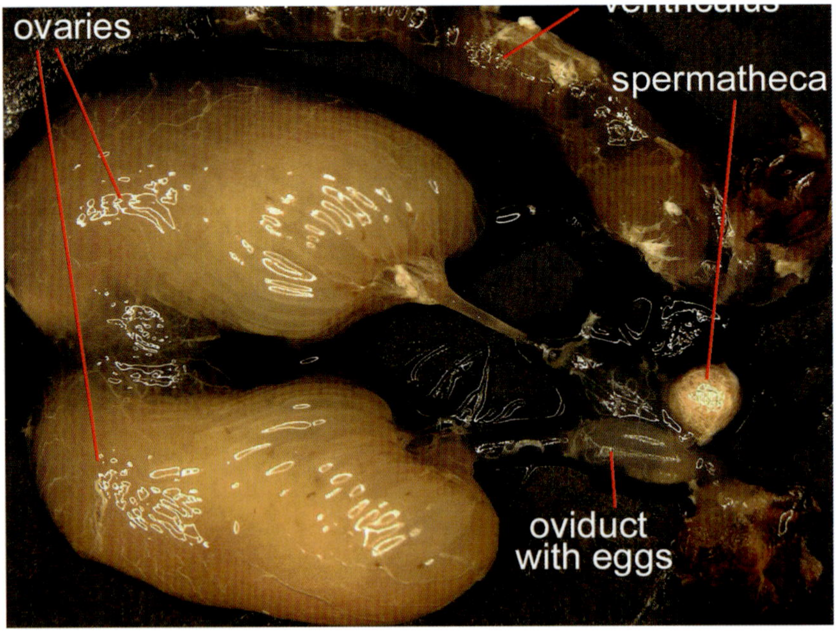

Here the structures are moved apart. Note the two ovaries connected to the oviduct by the laterial oviducts; developing eggs pass down these tubes to reach the spermatheca where sperm are released for fertilization.

side or 130 square inches for the full frame. Dividing that out, we get over nine frames containing brood. This realistically represents what we see in a normal colony during buildup.

If 1,500 eggs develop and emerge per day, the colony will generate 30,000 new bees over 20 days. At 3,500 bees per pound, this means that the queen has produced 8.5 pounds of new bees in a single brood cycle. I routinely reduce the egg laying rate by 10% during the spring buildup period (diploid drones), and 25% in the late summer/early fall due to increased worker cannibalism of eggs and larvae.

In the Starline/Midnite era of the 1970s we looked at egg-laying rates of hybrid queens open mated to unrelated drones and found that some queens were laying more than 1,500 eggs per day. Other queens and her bees produced over 1,700 eggs/day. Interestingly, these colonies were not the most productive in terms of honey production, as they seemed to consume more of the honey crop. This seems logical since they had the largest number of bees, but it may also indicate that the queen/bee interaction did not reduce egg laying when other colonies were reducing their rates due to declining conditions. This supports the theory that package bee producers select stock that produce the largest number of bees per day; but these stocks are often not the best honey producers when installed into colonies in northern apiaries.

There may be intensive periods of egg laying by queens supported by the bees in the hive, and I suspect that the daily egg-laying rate varies considerably due to weather, incoming food supplies, and the availability or lack of comb prepared by the workers for laying. If a brood nest is filled with brood, the cell cleaners and the queen must search throughout the colony for suitable places to place eggs. Sometimes she places two eggs into one worker cell, the pressure to lay is so great, and the prepared cells to put eggs are harder to find. This behavior often seen with new mated queens in smaller colonies and nucs. It must not be confused with egg-laying workers.

Number of bees in a hive

We can use these egg-laying rates to predict the theoretical number of bees in a colony. Since many scientists agree that during the spring and summer worker bees live up to six weeks after they emerge, so we need only double the bee production for one three week period and get 63,000 bees in our theoretical colony. That is about 18 pounds of bees, the equivalent of six three-pound packages of bees in a single hive, an impressive number. To be honest, it has been a long time since I have seen a colony that strong since tracheal and varroa mites arrived in America. If adult worker bees only live an average of four weeks (due to mite predation, etc.) the colony will have a potential of only 42,000 bees.

There are reports of up to 3,000 eggs produced per day over an extended period in certain colonies. For this to be correct, the bees must approach a colony population of 126,000 bees, with a total bee weight of 36 pounds, and the brood must cover between 12 to 18 frames, depending on the brood pattern. This is impossible, right?

This *might* happen if there are two queens laying eggs in one colony—mother and daughter laying side by side during the spring buildup period. I have observed as many as fifteen percent of all spring colonies with two or more queens. These mother and daughter queens were apparently undergoing a gradual supersedure, with a significant overlap of the laying activity of the two queens laying eggs in the same hive, and sometimes on the same side of the same brood comb. Research shows that worker bees tolerate gradually failing queens (without starting the queen replacement process) until her egg production falls to about half of the peak level. With a gradual decline in brood rearing, the old queen is allowed to exist in the colony after her daughter starts laying eggs. This keeps a laying queen in the hive in the event the daughter fails to mate, return to the hive, and initiate laying. The workers do not starve, reject or kill her, but accept her contribution to the egg laying of the newly mated daughter queen. The combined pheromone production of the two queens has not been examined as far as I am aware but I suspect the daughter queen is controlling the colony's pheromonal output, while the failing mother queen produces just enough pheromone to prevent her rejection/elimination by the workers.

There must be a strong evolutionary advantage when the old queen continues to produce eggs, even at a reduced rate. A colony able to produce a huge population of bees can generate multiple swarms, so two queens working together increases the survival

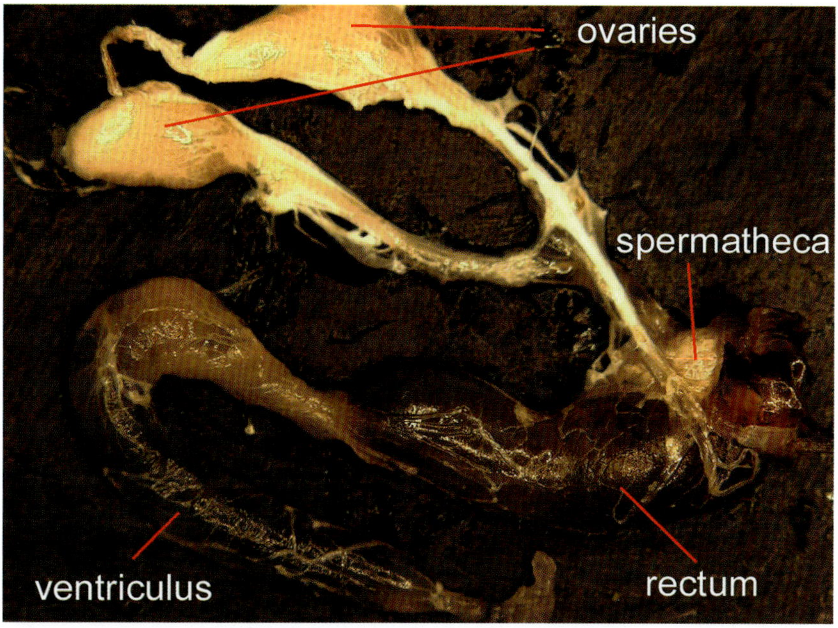

When a queen has been caged and held in a queen bank for some time, the eggs are absorbed and the ovaries shrink, reducing pheromone production.

of the colony and its daughter swarms. Any swarms the colony produces represent maternal sexual reproduction at the colony level. Rather than reproduction of the individual queen, the bees are concerned with the biological process involved in reproducing the entire colony via swarming. Since the earliest swarms are usually the largest, they have the highest statistical chance of building a new nest, storing adequate food to overwinter, and in turn reach its first birthday. In nature only about one swarm in six accomplishes this feat.

Nest size, colony expansion and colony survival

Bee nests in hollow trees occupy between 15 and 80 liters (one liter=1.0567 liquid quart) in volume. Anything smaller is not large enough for a European colony to store 15 kg (34 lbs) of honey necessary to survive the winter.[10] A deep Langstroth hive body contains about 42 liters and a double deep hive contains 84 liters. Wintering in two deep hive bodies is providing a nest volume that is drastically larger than anything the bees select by themselves. This permits a much larger buildup than seen in natural hives.

[10] Seeley, Thomas D., 1985. *Honeybee Ecology. A study of adaptation in social life*. Princeton University Press.

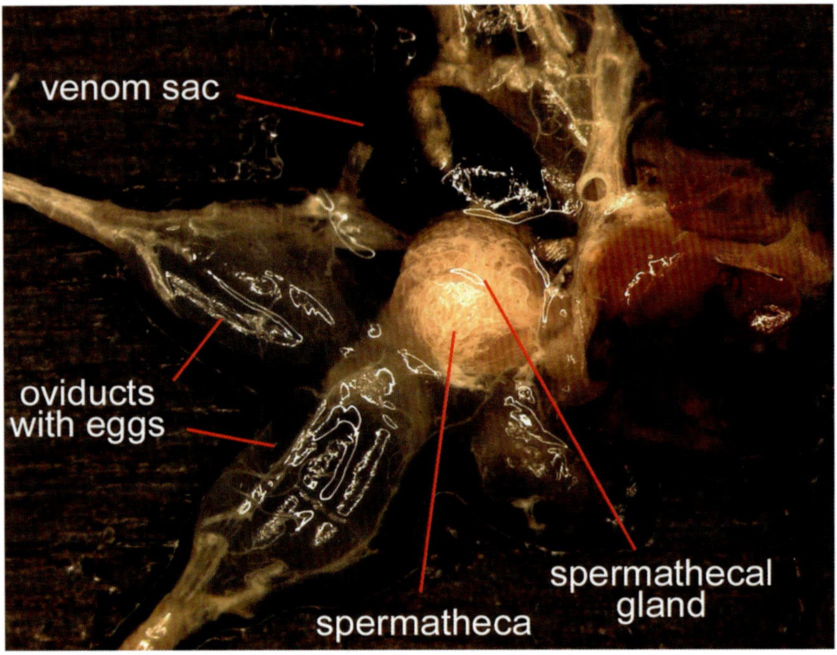

This is a close-up of the end of the reproductive tract, where the eggs that are being laid move out past the duct from the spermatheca.

When colonies experience very rapid buildup in the spring, the mass (weight) of bees, honey, pollen and wax comb increases from 10 to 20 kg in April (in the northern tier of states, earlier in southern states), to 65 to 75 kg by some point in July. During this interval a healthy colony will issue at least two swarms. Further swarms may weaken the colony's bee and food reserves too much, and the parent colony may not be strong enough to make it through the winter.

Swarms vary in size, but the average prime swarm is about 16,000 worker bees, the mother queen, and a few drones. In seven colonies monitored by Mark Winston, prime swarms ranged from 11,676 to 21,818 bees, secondary swarms ranged from 6,091 to 14,625 bees, and the two colonies that issued second afterswarms (for a total of three) were 3,765 and 4,086 bees. Finally, one colony produced a third afterswarm (total of four) with 4,296 bees[11]. From this, beekeepers should realize that the colonies that produced afterwarms take two risks: the smaller swarms probably will NOT survive to reach their first birthday, and the parent colony may

[11] Winston, Mark. 1987. *Biology of the Honey Bee*, Harvard University Press.

have depleted its own bee and resource supply to an extent that it too is less likely to grow one more season. This is balanced by the chance, however large or small, that the maternal reproduction of the colony via swarming will pass on the colony's genetics to two to more daughter swarms, a dramatic increase for a social unit like *Apis mellifera*.

Because it takes a queen laying 1,500 eggs per day one full brood cycle to produce 30,000 bees, a swarm of 16,000 workers represents about half of one cycle. Since half of all colonies also issue a second swarm (first afterswarm), some of which that are nearly as large as the prime swarm, such swarming behavior represents

Do worker bees manage the queen? Does the queen control the workers? Or do they interact and manage each other?

Brood pattern of a Russian colony in June showing few missed cells, indicating little inbreeding. Genetic control of colony buildup delay growth in the spring, but when it starts it is explosive.

one month's labor at peak season for the bee colony—labor represented by lost food reserves and worker bees. For the beekeeper it means that a month of prime buildup is missed—lost bee population, pollination service, and lost honey and pollen production. Also, during the swarming process bee reduce their foraging rate, and more bees are 'hanging out' in the hive and not gathering food. This is not a month lost over a twelve month calendar, but a month lost during the critical buildup/nectar gathering cycle.

Natural colonies rarely, if ever, reach 3,000 eggs per day or 126,000 bees in the hive. Beekeepers come closest to these numbers when they employ a *two-queen management system*, a highly desirable queen management and manipulation scheme that increases colony size and replaces the queen while reducing the swarming instinct.

Who is in charge of the hive?

Beekeepers often speak that the "queen" did this or that, but it is not accurate to say this. The queen follows her own instincts, nearly all of which require the full cooperation and support of the worker bees. For example, to lay eggs, a queen bee does not clean worker cells before she lays into them—the workers do this as part of their job. The queen does what she is allowed and stimulated to do by the worker bees from the moment they determine that a particular worker larva will become a future queen candidate in a developing queen cell. The workers may even confine a ready-to-emerge queen in her cell to keep her from killing her sister queens during the swarm season. During the daily life in a hive, workers control the rate of queen feeding and the number of worker cells prepared for her to lay into, thus controlling the queen's egg laying rate. This is one reason why stock evaluation tests should only be done when the queen has produced her own worker bees and replaced the old bees in the hive. Not only do you need to evaluate the queen in a hive, but you must evaluate the collective behaviors of the queen and her worker daughters.

One clearly independent act of the queen is in mating. The worker bees do not fly out on her mating flight, and they do not select which drones to be her mating partners. She selects the drones—or the queen and the drones select each other. Since a normal queen mates many times, she lets each successful drone fall to the ground one after another, each paralyzed and unable to fly. At the end of the mating flight the queen returns to the hive with part of the last drone's endophallus in her reproductive tract. Immediately the worker bees attend to her and remove the male tissue. They also remove thin stings of surplus seminal fluids as she passes them from her body—without this help it is doubtful the queen would every lay a single egg!

Old queens

Adrian Wenner[12] wrote me about his observation about old queens and theories of sperm storage. For a number of years he has been working with Catalina Island's feral bee population. The Island is part of a nature preserve that seeks to remove all non-native flora and fauna. Since honey bees are not native to the Americas, this means the honey bees must go too (a curious and perhaps unenlightened viewpoint, but, then, I was not consulted). He reported to me that there were at least two long-existing colonies with very old queens on the island. He also cited reports from a 1960 Russian abstract of queens being reported as old as nine years.

Commercially motivated beekeepers tend to requeen every year

[12]University of California, Santa Barbara, Emeritus Professor

or every other year. Some do so without fail, for they have learned the economic advantage of young vigorous queens. Others are less inclined to requeen colonies if the queen seems to be doing the job we expect.

For several years there have been reports of feral colonies able to maintain a separate genetic identity, even in areas of extensive commercial beekeeping. After the tracheal and varroa mite invasions, there were reports of a few feral colonies persisting in areas where mites had killed all managed hives. The first conclusion people reach is that these feral colonies possess some special genetic resistance to the mites. But it is also possible that the feral colonies have had minimal contact with the managed hives. Because of their relative isolation, the bees experienced minimal contact with each other in terms of drifting drone migration, mating differences and robbing. If the bees are of different genetic heritage, they may demonstrate floral foraging preferences. That the feral colonies may have been avoiding contact with managed colonies—and their varroa mites—by various biological isolation techniques.

We can speculate about these potential survivor colonies. Were they just lucky to avoid the mites, or do the mites respond differently to bees in isolated situations than in large apiaries? This was recently demonstrated by Tom Seeley in relatively isolated colonies in the Arnot Forest, outside of Ithaca. It appears that the mites adapt a different reproductive strategy when the number of host colonies is limited. It is not a good evolutionary strategy for a parasite to kill off *all* of its hosts.

With the colonies on Catalina Island, perhaps these queens represent a genetic extreme—they maintain a very small brood nest during most of the year, storing food and using it cautiously, and building only moderate populations in the spring due to limited forage. Perhaps these very old queens do not produce a colony strong enough to swarm but strong enough to prevent supersedure replacement. It seems possible that bee colonies in small cavities may experience this. In this example, the colony may have abundant stores and thus was not stimulated to collect a larger food reserve. How many eggs does a queen need to lay per day to maintain herself as queen and not be either swarmed out or superseded? The answer to this question could shed light on this complex nexus in determining the fate of the queen and her colony.

Some subspecies and strains of honey bees are well known for being conservative users of food reserves. In Florida I worked with a Carniolian-based line that were remarkably sensitive to the end of the nectar flow, and shut off egg-laying within a day (This is the F line discussed in Section IV). The USDA imported Russian ecotypes are both criticized and praised for their ability to delay buildup until the flow begins (but then exploding with growth).

Two colonies—And their possible performance

Let's compare two specific colonies. The first is a three-pound package newly installed on all new equipment and wax or plastic foundation. The second is new swarm, a prime swarm with a two-year old queen that finds an old bee nest in a tree where the former colony died due to starvation. Both colonies start with 12,000 bees, a queen and a few hundred drones.

The package colony must immediately begin comb construction. It will produce about one square meter of comb (ten square feet) in its first year if it is to survive. To achieve this it will metabolize about one-eighth of the honey it collects over the season to produce the beeswax needed for comb building. Bees that might otherwise forage for pollen and nectar are working on the task of wax secretion and comb building. The colony builds nicely because the queen is young, healthy and has not been exposed to miticides during her production. Unfortunately if the bees used in the package were shaken from a colony with a developing varroa mite population, the new colony will have mites reproducing at increasing rates in both drone and worker brood.

The swarm colony experiences good fortune by finding previously constructed and empty comb, so all the resources that would otherwise be required to build comb may now be put into foraging activities. There will be some comb repair and expansion, of course. The queen lays the brood nest filled with eggs and keeps the colony's population growing all season. The colony obtains enough forage to pack the brood nest with pollen and honey, and enters the winter with a low mite load if the source colony had a low mite level, and because by swarming the colony has experienced a break in mite rearing. Finally, the smaller colony usually produces fewer drones during its first season.

In the second season, the beekeeper pushes the package colony for honey production, and the original queen is replaced through

Swarm on a beautiful spring day. Swarming represents a huge risk for both the parent colony and the swarm itself—only one out of six swarms reaches its first birthday. Changes in queen pheromone levels promotes swarming; they are also key to the movement of the swarm to a new nest site.

supersedure during the spring buildup. While this created a break in the brood cycle, it probably stimulated the colony to produce many drones. Since varroa reproduces about three times faster in drone brood than worker brood, there is a rapid increase in varroa mite load and eventually colony collapsed during the late fall due to the mite infestation.

In its second season, the swarm colony starts the spring with large food reserves and the queen, now in her third year. She has reduced her egg laying rate by one third, not enough to cause her replacement, but enough to keep the colony from building to the point where it will swarm. In fact, the colony finds itself in a position where the queen and the size of the comb are well balanced, and the colony continues for several years this way, with the same queen and her reduced brood rearing.

The point of this comparison is to show that it is possible to have queens that appear to be just survivor stock—but vigorous survivor stock—possessing some unique genetic traits enabling the hive to survive mite attacks. What really happened was partly luck and partly situation. If the colony had not found the bee nest with pre-constructed comb, if it has not started with a low mite load, if the queen had not started to fail her third season—all these "ifs" created this unique but illustrative scenario for colony survival.

Adrian Wenner's comments help illustrate useful concepts of colony survival, especially the vast difference between the biological needs of a new colony in a beekeeper's operation compared to those of a lucky swarm established in the wild.

Understanding queen pheromones

Queen chemicals (pheromones)

To understand queen bees and their role in the beehive, we need to have a working knowledge of the chemicals produced by bees, especially by queens, and how they create changes within the hive. These chemicals are pheromones, from the Greek *pherein*, to transfer and *hormon*, to excite. These chemicals are produced by one individual, released into the environment, and cause a change in another individual member of the same species. They start as liquids produced by specialized cells or glands and enter the environment as liquids or gases. The excitement or change they cause in another individual is species specific. In honey bees, pheromones are involved in the complex and diverse behaviors of mating, swarming, brood rearing, ovary suppression and more.

Pheromonal systems are common in many animals, especially in insect species. They are found in mammals where they are linked with sexual attraction and arousal. They are also linked to mother-newborn interactions. Of all the pheromone systems yet studied, the system at work in the bee hive colony is the most complex.

What are the queen's pheromones?

Information about the queen bee's pheromone is growing, and we will concentrate on these chemicals and their impact on bees. The queen mandibular pheromone (QMP) is often called the *queen substance*, a term given to it by Dr. Colin Butler in 1954. The primary component is 9-oxydec-2-enoic acid, commonly called 9-ODA. This chemical was isolated from the mandibular glands of queen bees. These glands are connected by a duct that connects to the mandibles of the queen. There are two glands, one for each mandible.

The chemical we call queen substance is actually 17 different compounds that have been isolated from mandibular glands. Dr. Dewey Caron, in his textbook *Honey Bee Biology and Beekeeping*, lists five molecules as the "most important". These five molecules work together, and the removal of any one of them cuts the level of "excitement" by half. The first three molecules are acids, and the last two are aromatic compounds:

9-ODA	9-oxydec-2-enoic acid
9-HDA	cis-9-hydroxydec-2-enoic acid

Attendant bees change as the queen walks over the combs, most touching their antennae to the queen's body. Others use their tongue to touch, feed. groom, or remove wastes from the queen.

9-HDA trans-9-hydroxydec-2-enoic acid
HOB methyl-p-hydroxyenzoate
HVA 4-hydroxy-3-methoxyphenylethanol

These molecules and their role as pheromones were discovered in a series of research projects conducted since 1961. Work continues to discover other ways these molecules are utilized as part of the queen pheromone blend.

Queen retinue pheromone

A laying queen honey bee apparently performs two major functions in the colony. Ideally, she will oviposit about 200,000 eggs into worker and drone cells over a year, serving as the biological mother of all the bees in the hive, passing her genes to her daughter queens and her drone sons. Second, she is the producer of pheromones from glands in her body.

In 2003 we learned more about the concept of the queen retinue pheromone, which allows other molecules from the queen's body to contribute to the behavior we see in bees that visit, groom her, feed her, and receive her pheromone in the process[13]. Most beekeepers have watched the queen when surrounded by her retinue of nurse worker bees. This occurs when the queen is resting from egg laying. During active egg laying the retinue does not exist or is poorly defined. The bees in the retinue are constantly changing, some only make brief contact with the queen with their antennae, during which pheromones are passed from queen to worker. These workers are then in an "excited" mode, carrying the pheromone throughout the hive to other workers. This spreads the chemicals throughout the colony so all bees are aware of the queen's presence even though most of them have not had physical contact with her.

Other retinue workers lick the queen's body and obtain pheromone, while others feed and others remove her feces. The queen rectum produces pheromone and pheromone-loaded feces are found in other animals. This includes the only mammal with a queen, one that suppresses her daughters reproduction by pheromones in her feces, the naked mole rat of Africa.

The same Simon Fraser team measured the amount of these dif-

[13]Keeling, Slessor, Higo and Winston, New components of honey bee (*Apis mellifera* L) queen retinue phermone. PNAS, Simon Fraser University.

ferent chemicals produced by mated, laying queens. They call this blend of pheromone a *queen equivalent* (Qeq):

Chemical	Amount
9-ODA	~200 micrograms
9-HDA (both forms)	80 micrograms
HOB	20 micrograms
HVB	2 micrograms

A queen secretes one Qeq every 24 hours. She moves the pheromone to other parts of her body by her self-grooming and by worker grooming. Virgin queens produce significantly less 9-HDA, HOB and undetectable amounts of HVA. As a result, virgin queens are much less attractive to worker bees. Once mated and laying eggs, the queens are fully attractive to the bees in the colony. This helps us understand how virgin queens are relatively free to move around the colony until they are mated. Since they do produce *some* of the Qeq, beekeepers must treat them much the same as a mated queen; they cannot be dropped into a foreign colony and be expected to survive.

Genes control queen pheromone production

Different queens differ in their queen mandibular pheromone due to different genes they possess. Breeders selected for high or low producers of the queen mandibular pheromone and the high QMP strain produced nine times more pheromone than the low strain.[14]

In the strain with low QMP production, the bees still responded to the queen in a normal manner, suggesting there are other molecules produced by the queen that added to the queen retinue response by worker bees. Pheromones were moved from the head to the tergite gland in the top of the queen's abdomen.

Four new retinue molecules

As other researchers examined the queen retinue pheromone, they found four new molecules that work in synergy with QMP to excite workers. The nine compounds do not combine to provide the same retinue response of queen extract at higher doses, suggesting that still more molecules are yet to be discovered. The four new molecules are[15]:

[14]Pankiw, T., Winston, M.L. Fondrk, M.K. Slessor, K.N. 2000. Selection on honey bee responses to queen pheromone (*Apis mellifera* L.). Naturwissenschaften 87:487-490

[15]Keeling et al., 2003. New components of the honey bee (*Apis mellifera* L.) queen retinue pheromone, PNAS, Vol 10:8

methyl oleate	methyl (A)-octadec-9-enoate
Coniferyl alcohol	(E)-3-hydroxy-3methoeyt-phenyl)proop-2-en-1-ol
Heyadecane-1-ol	
Linolenic acid	(Z9,Z12, z15)-octa-dexa-9, 12, 15-trienoic acid

These pheromones are produced in different glands in the queen's body, and their production may be influenced by the metabolism of each gland. Some molecules are found on the queen that previously were found on honey bee brood, suggesting that the queen works to control worker physiology and behavior, and regulates retinue bees in the amount they lick, antennate, and groom her. This implies that the queen controls more of the behavior of the bees than previously thought, at least in getting someone to pay attention to her.

Queen perfection

Once I attended a meeting in a southern state where bee geneticist Walter Rothenbuhler of The Ohio State University spoke to a group of about 35 commercial honey bee queen propagators. At a key

The first step in queen production—by beekeepers—is to select the smallest well-fed larva of the right age. The center larvae does not have enough royal jelly, while the larva in the lower right is too large.

point in his talk, Rothenbuher asked each participant to speak out the "most important characteristic" they wanted in their queens. I was pretty innocent then to the ways and politics of beekeepers and figured there would be two or three characteristics that they would all agree as being the "most" important aspect of a queen bee.

As the propagators went around the room, my eyes were opened. Each one of them voiced a *different* characteristic (of both queen and her colony) until a total of 32 items were crammed onto the dusty chalk board. One wanted a high egg-laying queen while another said it was 'most' important to easily find the queen in the hive. There were many ideas in between. I mention this because it is difficult, if not completely impossible, to define what queen perfection is for any particular beekeeper. Some consider egg laying rate to be the ultimate consideration, especially if the beekeeper shakes bees for packages or makes increase colonies in the spring and must have huge amounts of brood and numbers of bees. Yet the northern beekeeper seeks a bee hive that survives the winter and builds quickly in the spring to produce a spring honey crop. Another beekeeper who experienced huge disease or mite losses

This is a broodless, flightless starter box improvised from a double nucleus box. Nurse bees from healthy colonies were shaken into the box and the cell bars positioned next to pollen and honey frames and a water soaked sponge.

almost will insist that colonies have resistance to bee diseases and parasitic mites, even at the "cost" of reduced honey production.

Unusual requests appear: One beekeeper who focused on bees for pollination wanted queens that produced workers resistant to common pesticides, but immediately honey producers took strong exception to the idea. What would happen if colonies resisted common agricultural insecticides and survived with residues in the hive or honey? This might ruin the entire honey industry. Most beekeepers agreed that colonies should be good honey producers, but not all. Some wanted high pollen collectors to insure their effectiveness as crop pollinators. Clearly, queen perfection is a very personal concept, and any attempt to provide one bee stock that everyone can use is met with extreme criticism for what it cannot do.

Queen vigor: Theory vs. reality

To understand queen perfection we must clearly differentiate between genetic perfection and the conditions of queen production. During Rothenbuhler's talk, the group discussed the varied

Confined to the starter box overnight, the cells should be well covered with bees. Accepted cells will have wax added to the edge of the cell and abundant royal jelly around the larvae.

conditions under which queens are produced, and the stresses queens are subjected to before they are installed into a hive or nucleus. Everyone agreed that queens must be able to withstand the rigors of being mailed or shipped to customers. They should not—in theory—experience supersedure for at least two years and must produce solid brood patterns of worker brood. They should be sensitive to feeding, flows and other conditions and adjust brood rearing accordingly. Swarming should be rare. The colony should not sting, be conservative in using food resources, and must produce peak bee populations able to pollinate crops and collect nectar for top honey production.

These traits mix two separate situations in the queen rearing business. Some traits are genetically controlled, while others rely upon the conditions of queen production. Genetic traits include egg laying rates, tendency toward swarming, number of stings received per hive visit and a full range of bee behaviors. These traits are not removed by conditions of poor queen rearing, but may be masked by them. So we need to review conditions critical to the production of a perfectly produced queen. Even if we have all the genetic traits we want in a queen, they may be masked by poor rearing and mating conditions. Many queen propagators do a very good job of producing very well reared and mated queens but are using stock that may not carry all the traits beekeepers seek. Many commercial and sideline beekeepers accept this as a brutal reality of modern beekeeping.

Natural queen cells during swarm season. Look for long, well sculptured cells.

Size IS important!

Large queens are better because they contain more egg-producing structures called ovarioles, and, as a result, are able to lay more eggs within the same time period as a smaller queen from the same stock. Queens that lay more eggs have larger colonies and collect more nectar and pollinate more flowers.

Queens have two large ovaries, collectively holding between 260 and 373 ovarioles, based on a study of 280 queens by Eckert

Long, well sculptured queen cells produced by a "microbreeder". One cell is covered with wax comb due to the nectar flow. As queen cells mature, the pupae inside begin to produce queen pheromone.

in 1934. Each ovariole produces five to seven eggs per day, so a well reared queen is able to put between 1200 to 1500 eggs into queen cells every day during the critical spring buildup season. Since there are 1440 minutes in a 24-hr day, a queen produces an average of about one egg every sixty seconds. This is not a constant rate, but varies as the queen searches for prepared cells—there are periods of feeding, grooming, waste removal and rest for the queen. There is documentation of slightly higher egg laying rates, between 1500 to 1800 eggs per day. These bees produce such a large colony that additional food collection is rapidly consumed. This suggests that there is an optimization of colony size and egg laying rates. When you read reports of 2500 to 3000 eggs per day, look for a second queen, usually a daughter queen, laying in the same hive as her mother during colony build-up. Such "supersedure strains" possess an unique trait for rapid buildup in overwintered colonies.

Absolutely anything that interferes with the development of the queen and her eventual size will interfere with the size of the queen, the number of her ovarioles, and even the size of her spermatheca. I gave the example of the size of the spermatheca in the prior section.

Dr. G.H. "Bud" Cale, Jr., developer of the Starline and Midnite hybrid bees was a strong advocate for the production and use of large queens. His dissertion examined heterosis (hybrid vigor) in the honey bee. He spoke out against propagators who shipped queens that were too small. In addition to their reduced egg laying potential, they experienced poor introduction rates and were often superseded quickly.

Hybrid bees like Starline and Midnite bees (no longer available) demonstrated hybrid vigor (heterosis) and were physically larger than many non-hybrid lines. Their increased physical size added to their larger egg laying rate and foraging abilities.

The queens initially selected to create these hybrids were large queens, and through the inbreeding-hybridizing process, the resulting hybrid queens were larger than the parents and able to produce a large number of eggs. The loss of the availability of true hybrids may be one reason contributing to more frequent queen turnover in apiaries.

In his book, *Beekeeping for Beginners* (Journal Printing Company for Dadant and Sons, 1964), Cale shows a photo of three queens (page 96) and he evaluates them for size. The smallest was a very poor layer. She had a stubby body and her fully engorged abdomen reached just slightly beyond the tip of the forewing. The second queen had forewings that covered all but two segments of the queen's abdomen plus the tip. She is very typical of the queens I see in many apiaries. The third queen's forewings failed to cover the three last segments of the abdomen, and these were much more swollen, so that length of the forewing was just a little less than half the length of the engorged abdomen. When I worked in Florida, beekeepers there called these "gator" queens because they had such a long "tail." These queens are the result of excellent queen rearing conditions, proper feeding by nurse bees. They have the optimum number of ovarioles that produce the maximum number of eggs their genetics allow.

In nature such optimized queens are produced during the swarming season, when the colony undergoes division into two or more colonies. A queen produced under the swarming instinct is destined to become a queen *before* the egg is laid by the old queen in the queen cups. Think about it—all the factors favoring ideal

Strong cell-finishing (cell-builder) colonies at Koehnens in California.The large bee population and feed produce will-fed, quality queens.

queen production exist *before* the queen lays the egg—the colony population is high, food reserves are excellent, and the promise of continued growth stimulates the bees to produce queens from choice larvae, fed them profusely, and never allow them to become stressed. The colony only swarms if conditions favoring swarming continue during the developmental period.

At the other extreme we have queens produced under the emergency instinct. Something has happened to the old queen, and she must be immediately replaced. The colony is limited to only those larvae that are in the colony—they cannot wait for conditions to improve. Food reserves are those that are present, little can be done to improve stores during emergency replacement. There is even evidence that foraging reduces during queen replacement because there is a drop in the pheromone stimulation of foragers. The conditions for larval selection, cell building, feeding and stress on the queen and drones during this interval are often unknown. Certainly, you will not know what you will get—if anything—during emergency queen production.

There is a middle range of queen cell production. In nature this occurs when queens are being replaced by the supersedure process, a natural and totally instinctive time when the old queen's decline in pheromone production and reduced egg laying stimulates the bees to select larvae for new queen production.

Queen propagators attempt to mimic swarming conditions by providing abundant nurse bees, a large surplus of stored food

Bee population in a microbreeder's cell builder colony. This colony produced the cells seen on page 75.

and incoming food (provided by syrup feeding). The combs and colonies are ideal for cell production, flooded with bees and food. Young, healthy nurse bees consume abundant pollen and honey to produce a large amount of royal jelly to feed the developing queen larvae. Large populations manage temperatures precisely so there is no over or under heating of the developing cells. There cannot be too many old bees—they will web the cells together with burr comb during a nectar flow—they may be removed by moving the colony several feet and collecting the old foragers in a "dummy" hive filled with comb and a queen.

This way, whatever the genetic potential of the queen can be expressed at its maximum, helping promote queen introduction and success in the colony for several years.

Handle with care

Unfortunately, many well reared and mated queens are lost each year because they have been mishandled by the queen propagator, a shipping agent, or the receiving beekeeper. *Queen cells* must be handled like thin-shelled eggs. They must be handled at the base and never at the tip. Near the point of emergence, queen cells may be laid down onto cotton or soft fabric, and not be pinched or crowded. Wood and plastic cell bases provide additional cell production at this stage, and may be used to push the base of the cell into comb when introduced into a mating colony. Never pinch or bruise the tip of the cell as you handle and introduce a cell.

Never drop or shake cells because the larvae and developing pupa my be dislodged from its position on the royal jelly or in the cell and be injured. During active metamorphosis from pupae to adult, any sharp movement may cause deformities of the wings, legs, antennae, and other body parts.

Adult queens must always be picked up from the comb by their wings. When you seek to clip or mark a queen, hold her down with gentle finger pressure on the thorax, not the abdomen and then lift her by the wings. Do not hold the queen by a leg, as she will twist to get away—that inevitability leads to damage to the leg, and a queen with short tenure in the hive. Crushing the abdomen will result in damaged ovarioles and may interfere with egg laying. I recommend that beekeepers clip the tip of a queen's wing to identify her—paint marks wear and chip off over time. Clip the right wing in even years and the left wing in odd years. Then you know when the queen was introduced. Extreme wing removal will result in balance problems with the queen and supersedure.

Extremes in temperature, especially in mailing cages, has been shown to cause tragic results in queen success. Even though the queen may still be alive following exposure to 120 degrees F. it will interfere with her ability to survive introduction and the pressures of a new queen. Keep bees in conditions where you are comfortable. If you are hot or chilled, the queens may be as well.

Hydration is critical to bees in shipment and storage—any time the queen is not in the hive. Newly shipped queens should be given water on the screen of the mailing cage until the queen (and attendants, if there are any) fail to take any more. Return every few hours to put a small amount of water on the screen. Many shippers believe the queen candy contains enough moisture to maintain the queen. This is probably true for a brief period, but any caged queens confined over two days will clearly benefit from water.

Queen holding is easy if you plan to introduce new queens in the next 24-48 hours. A supply of clean water on the cage will provide what is necessary. Use an eyedropper to add water—your fingers may include anything from transmission fluid to hamburger grease. Longer queen holding will require you to make up a simple queen bank. For many beekeepers, the simplest queen bank is a four or five frame nucleus colony with two frames of bees and brood, a frame of pollen and a frame of honey. Either water or sugar syrup should be supplied according to the season.

An excellent queen bank for field work is a small cardboard box (cigar box) with a tight lid. I put 4 to 8 caged queens screen side up, and add a small water feeder (a piece of sponge soaked in water works well). To this I add a shake of nurse bees from a brood frame. The nurse bees will care for the queen and regulate temperatures as you take the box into the apiary (avoid direct sunlight), and into the local greasy spoon for lunch (rather than leave them in the car or truck). These bees may be kept this way for a day or two—if they start to smell like old sneakers shake off the old bees and add fresh nurse bees.

Finally rough handling of hives causes a lot of queen mortality—estimated between 5 and 15% every move. This may be acceptable for some commercial pollinators and honey producers, but cage valuable breeder stock before you move colonies.

During routine colony inspections avoid queen-damaging behaviors. Work from one side of the hive to the other, carefully

Low bee population and poor brood area indicate a problem in this post-almond bloom colony; such colonies are inferior for use in breeding work.

inspecting each frame and the frame appearing next in the box to see if the queen is present. Keep handy an empty hive shell or nucleus box to place a frame holding the queen as you continue your colony inspection. You don't want to put your foot through the comb holding the queen and accidentally kill her.

Always keep the queen in mind. Once, during a prolonged search for a queen, I felt a bee crawling up the inside of my pant-leg. I instinctively went to pinch the bee, but felt the larger size of the bee, and shook out the queen from my pants. This queen had been clipped and marked and I do not know what mission she was inside my jeans. She reentered her hive without comment.

Queen management

Records, clipping, marking

Good beekeepers are aware of the status of the queens in their colonies. It does not matter how you record data about your queens—pencil notes on the lid, a pocket notebook, laptop computer or a voice recording gadget—record what you see about the queen in every brood nest inspection. While you do not need or even want to see the queen on every hive visit, you should be able to identify her by her markings, or as a supersedure queen.

In breeding work we clipped the tip of the wing (not the majority of the wing) to confirm queen identification. Otherwise it was possible to have mistaken a daughter for her mother and lost valuable breeding information. We marked daughter queens as drone mothers following documented supersedures.

Only if you are grafting from a particular queen do you need to physically see her (and no others) laying on the combs on a regular basis. Evidence of the queen is seen in the constant production of eggs and new brood in a hive. If you have normal worker eggs in the bottoms of cells, you are assured the queen is present and doing her job.

In our record keeping we measured queen performance in terms of tenths of a frame of worker and drone brood. As we worked a colony we mentally computed the frames of bees and brood. Any developing queen failure was noted and corrected.

Supersedure

We traditionally think queen supersedure takes place every two to five years when the old queen fails. Unfortunately that is not the case with aggressively managed colonies. There are supersedures soon after new queens are successfully introduced—they are rejected within a few weeks of acceptance as cells are constructed. Studies show that poor queen rearing conditions, extremes in heat, cold during mail or trucking, and beekeeper inexperience often lead to early replacement of the new queen.

Some strains of bees are quick to produce queen cells. The Russian stock is known for having queen cells throughout the buildup season, but that does not mean that they are producing swarms or replacement queens. It may be part of their increased tolerance against the varroa mites (why they were introduced into this country) and I am sure we do not fully understand or appreciate these different behaviors.

A queen that is poorly produced or exposed to heat, cold or pesticides will often be replaced early in her life. If the colony is otherwise building nicely, cut out any queen cells and often the new queen will get through the supersedure process of the colony and live a normal life. But if the new queen does not have much brood, and certainly if there are no signs of egg laying, then the bees should be helped to replace the queen.Add a frame of emerging brood from another colony to insure maintenance of a healthy population of nurse bees. Or combine the colony with the queen problem on a good colony to consolidate the bees.

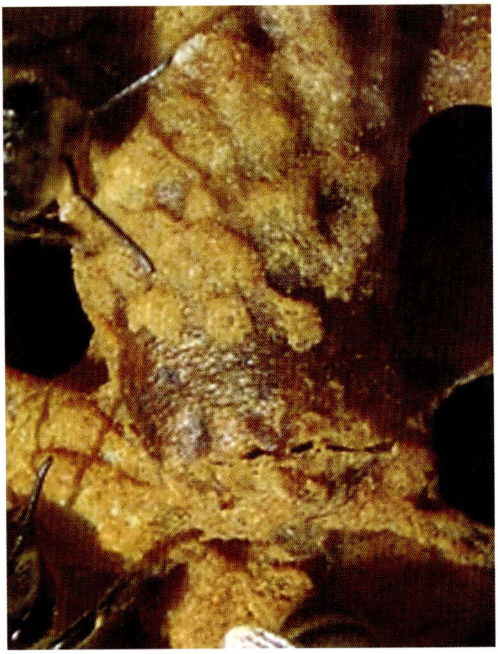

Detecting the pheromones produced by the queen, the workers have removed wax down to the cocoon. As the queen starts to cut her way out, the workers may "hold" her in the cell by adding wax to the opening.

Drone layers

Queens that have not been mated, or queens that have run out of sperm, or queens that mated to drones that were exposed to certain miticides—all may lead to a healthy queen producing drone brood. Most of this brood is in worker cells, since the queen and bees do not 'know' these eggs are unfertilized. The most common cause of drone layers in colonies is the harvesting of a queen from a mating nucleus before she has mated. While this would seem to be a simple matter of record keeping, it is apparent that there are frequent errors. It may result after a period of rainy weather during which the virgins could not fly. Or it may happen when a mating nucleus gets 'off cycle' with the other mating colonies and has produced its own queen—the infamous "side comb virgin" rather than accept the queen cell that was introduced into the unit.

Drone layers are often produced after the weather has been cold and wet, and the virgins have been unable to take their mating flights. Also, this happens when there are no drones mature enough to be present in the drone congregation areas, and the virgins have nothing to show for their efforts in the air, laying unfertilized eggs after 21-28 days post emergence. These conditions may also result in queens that are *under-mated*, having stored only a small fraction of the sperm in their spermatheca needed to maintain a normal colony. In this situation, the queens often start to lay drone eggs at the end of their first season, or in the start of the next.

The best treatment for a drone laying colony is to kill the offensive queen and combine the hive with a strong colony, where the bees will be of some benefit. A stronger colony will sort out the drones developing in the worker combs and all will be corrected in a few days. Do not requeen colonies with drone laying queens unless a nucleus with a laying queen is added to re-establish the colony. By placing a nucleus with a laying queen in the center of a defective colony, there is increased chance of ultimate success.

Queen handling and injury

Accidents

Inside the hive queens are subjected to accidents and injury during development, as they emerge from their cells, and from competitive sister queens. Outside the hive things are not much better, being subject to injury of death while on their mating flight, orientation errors during flights, and in rare events that endanger the bee nest (fire, falling trees). Most queen injury is a result of beekeeper error and mishandling during shipment. Here are concerns beekeepers must keep in mind whenever a queen fails.

Pesticides inside and outside the hive

Queens may be exposed directly to chemicals used by beekeepers to control mites and diseases of the hive. Apistan, coumophos, formic acid, thymol, are chemicals foreign to queen development and biology, or are used in much larger amounts than found in nature. Several compounds, such as coumophos, harm queens even when used at recommended amounts, or when the chemical is present in the hive for a prolonged time period. Chemical exposure has been lined to new queen introduction problems, early queen replacement, a tendency toward drone layers, and other problems.

Among the chemicals recommended for use inside the hive, there have been few studies that have examined the synergistic effect when multiple miticides are applied within the same hive, either at the same time or from residual effects. Very little is known when pesticides from outside the hive are added to the hive's contaminates—certainly the potential for queen damage increases. The area of queen damage (and to drones and workers) from synergistic chemical exposure is lacking, and is an area where researchers are needed to help the beekeeping industry. Contaminated combs also impact queen and drone viability and should be removed as part of a regular 3 or 5 year comb rotation.

Diseases

Diseases like the foulbroods and chalkbrood do not affect queen larvae because queens develop quicker than workers or drones. The queen's shorter developmental time also prevents varroa mite reproduction on queen larva. There are, however, unique diseases for queens. One is the black cell disease, a virus that kills queen larvae and turns the queen cells dark in color. A fungus is passed from drones to virgin queens during mating. These diseases are rare, but will be seen in any large scale queen cell production business.

Queen finding and introduction

To find a queen in a colony, work when the colony is at its smallest population for the season. This is often during the springtime, or after an increase nucleus colony has been made and given a queen or queen cell. While I have attempted to find queens in large colonies with two or more brood boxes, my success rate is sometimes low, and my frustration level was pretty high. Colonies with less than ten frames of brood are much easier to examine for a queen.

In the field use an empty hive body when looking for a queen. Place the cover (and inner cover) on the ground, having examined them for the queen. The empty box is placed on the cover. Carefully remove the outside or next-to-outside comb, and systematically remove the frames, examining each one by rotating it top to bottom and back again, using your eyes to scan for the queen. Look for the thickness of the queen that is a function of her egg laying. This "dorsal-ventral" swelling is unique in the bees, and once your eyes are trained, is easy to spot. When queens hide in the corners and cracks of the combs, this thickness may be the only characteristic we may use.

Look ahead at the next frame, still in the hive, as you work. Since a queen may seem negatively phototactic (move away from open spaces), she will undoubtedly move to the dark part of the hive. If you look at the next frame in a hive before you examine the one in your hands, you may catch sight of the queen before she hides under a layer of worker bees. Work through the frames of a hive and then returned them to the box, inspecting them in both directions. Stop if you have not found the queen and return to this hive later that same day or on a future day or take more drastic action, like shaking all the bees through a queen excluder.

Large populations of bees—When dealing with a large colony that must be requeened (they are often the ones with added defensive behavior), visit the apiary at least four days before the inspection and place queen excluders between each hive body. In that way you will have the queen confined within one hive body as evidenced by the eggs in the cells. This way you only have nine or ten frames to inspect rather than every frame in the colony.

Shaking or blowing out bees—When some commercial beekeepers remove their honey they shake or blow out the bees (using a bee blower) off all frames, and into the area in front of the hive. A piece of queen excluder is placed at the entrance of each hive to prevent the queen from reentering. She should be found and killed at the entrance. This also keeps out drones. A new queen is installed into the hive using a push in cage so she will be confined for several days before she is released when the colony has settled down considerably. This system does not work well with equipment that has broken edges and old hive bodies. Seal up the cracks and any gaps with duct tape if necessary to prevent the old queen from entering the hive.

Queen introduction tips

The Benton and plastic cages are used extensively to ship queen to beekeepers. They are widely used for queen introduction as well—beekeepers place the cages between two frames of brood after removing the cork or plug at the candy end of the cage. They check the candy to make sure it is not too hard, but should not use a nail to pierce the candy unless they want to speed the queen's release. Rapid queen release of queens often results in queen rejection. Here are some suggestions for increased queen acceptance:

Delayed release of queens—Beekeepers who want to use the cage the queen was shipped in, and not transfer her into another introduction device, should do so with great care. Instead of removing the cork in the candy end of the cage, cover both corks (or leave the plastic plug closed) with a staple or duct tape and position cage between brood frames in the center of the brood nest of the hive. Leave the queen in the cage for four to seven days. On a return visit to the hive, remove the tape or staple from the candy end, remove the cork, and soften the candy a bit so the queen will be released. Or direct release the queen by pulling the screen off the shipping cage, taking care not to damage the queen. Allow the queen to walk out of the cage and on to the brood frame. Her behavior should be normal, and the bees may seem to ignore her. Often she will go to a honey cell and take a long drink. Gently put the frame back into the hive and do not disturb her for several days so she starts laying normally.

Some beekeepers report that when they direct release the queen she may fly out of the cage or off the frame. If this happens just leave everything the way it is and allow the queen time to return to the area and land on the frame. This does not always happen, and you may find your new queen in a neighboring colony! When queens fly like this they are still small, and not swollen with eggs. It is possible the queen may still be a virgin, which is really upsetting if you thought you purchased a mated queen.

Push-in cages—There are plastic push-in cages on the market used for introducing queens. In the past I made them from a 5 inch x five inch piece of 8 mesh (or finer) hardware cloth. This is cut and folded

Plastic push in cage. The cage is pressed against an area of emerging worker brood that care for the queen (she is introduced through the opening). After confinement for 4-7 days to mix her odor in the hive, the queen is released.

so the cage has "feet" that push into the brood comb and enclose the queen without pinching her. I select a frame of brood where bees are emerging, and put the queen and cage over that. The newly emerged bees are not biased against the queen, and will feed her with the food they receive through the cage. The queen is on brood comb, and may start laying. In one corner of the cage is a metal or plastic tube that is filled with softened queen candy. Failing that I have rolled queen candy as a cylinder shape and wrapped it in a small sheet of waxed paper. After the bees remove the candy (and paper), the queen is free to enter the entire hive. By then the bees in the cage have helped distribute her pheromone odor to the rest of the colony. The cage itself may be removed on the next hive visit, and has not changed the spacing of frames.

Requeening a large colony with a nucleus containing a laying queen—Many successful beekeepers keep one or two nucleus colonies in each apiary, representing at least ten percent of the colony count in a larger operation. The nucleus colonies provide a resource of laying queens that do not need to be caged, shipped and delivered. Many beekeepers find that they may use the entire nucleus as a means of requeening a colony with problems (drone layers, laying workers, high defensiveness). In the colony to receive the nucleus, outside frames are removed, and space for the nucleus frames is made in the center of the brood nest. The nucleus frames with brood and the queen are gently put into the space. The colony is closed and fed sugar syrup. Removed frames may be placed into the nucleus and, if brood is present, used to reestablish the nucleus by adding a queen cell, virgin or mated queen.

Feeding during requeening—Unless there is a strong nectar flow underway, I recommend feeding the colony that is being requeened. This engorges the bees and makes them less likely to act negatively toward the new queen. If I know I have colonies to requeen in advance, I add feed to the colony three to five days in advance of the queen's introduction. It is a small insurance effort to protect valuable queens.

Queen storage banks

Surplus queens may be kept in a queen bank until needed. The longest I have banked a queen is nine months, and the queens performed within normal limits. Ordinarily I recommend storing queens for no more than a few weeks. Banks are routinely used by large scale queen propagators to hold an inventory of queens beyond the normal production season. This is especially true when propagators use very small mating units such as the mini nucleus. These units are being replaced with larger nuclei because they are easily destroyed by small hive beetles.

Recently research has shown that queens perform best if held in a nucleus or queen bank until the queens are at a least a month old. Since most queen propagators harvest queens on 14, 17 or 21 day intervals, they will need to rely on queen banks for the difference in the holding period.

A queen bank is an artificially queenless colony or a cell-builder like colony where the hive's queen is confined below a queen excluder. In either system two or more frames of brood surround a special frame that holds the shipping or storage cages. When set up the bank MUST be given a large number of young nurse bees. This is one of the keys to successful banking. Otherwise all the stored queens may die of neglect. On a weekly or ten-day interval add frames of emerging brood to keep up the population of young bees. Feed the colony at all times with a thin sugar syrup containing medication for nosema. If not, the nosema levels will build up in the queen's midgut and they will be short-lived, facing an early supersedure.

When we banked queens during the Starline/Midnite program we wondered what changes took place in the queens. We had many thousands of queens in banks at all times during the season. We found that good queen banks were hard to keep strong, and they required the most intensive management of any of the colonies

Typical home-made frame to hold about 60 queens in Benton mailing cages in the queenless region of a hive set up like a cell finisher colony. Remove all attendants. Position the cage screen out, but so the candy end of the cage is down and the queen has full exposure to the workers in order to feed her. Place between two frames of brood in the queen holder colony. At all times feed with syrup medicated to prevent Nosema in the hive. Keep the colony filled with nurse bees by adding frames of emerging worker brood.

dedicated to queen or drone production. We experienced problems with certain queens being taken care of better than others. As a result we kept *same with same*, in other words, young queens with young queens, and older mated queens with older mated queens. We found that there were some of the inbred lines that were favored by the bees while others were ignored and often died from neglect. When I left the breeding program in late 1980 I felt the primary reason we were unable to successfully mass produce instrumentally inseminated queens had a great deal to do with our lack of knowledge about queen banking. Any effort to repeat our effort at mass production of II queens must address these challenges.

Since our typical queen banks had 60-120 mated queens stored above a laying queen (over an excluder) I was concerned about the pheromone (queen substance) production by each queen in storage. Some queens died while in the bank as if they were being ignored by the workers. Recently USDA researcher Diana Sammataro indicated that the queens in these banks stop producing queen pheromone. This is cautionary to all beekeepers who purchase banked queens, because any queen from such a bank will require several days to become a healthy pheromone producer once introduced into a colony. Holding queens in a cage for 5-7 days should allow the bees to feed her adequately to return pheromone production to a normal level.

Our methods of running the Starline/Midnite program, which depended on banked queens, provided an additional selection pressure on the queens. While I looked at a dead queen as selection against lack of vigor or healthiness, perhaps our program was selecting only for their ability to survive under the conditions of queen storage, and these traits had little to do with the ones we sought in our general breeding program. Perhaps a successful breeding program must have all queens in nucleus colonies to maximize their potential in a normalized environment. This will increase costs considerably.

Queen banks must be worked every 7-10 days. Remove combs as they are filled with honey and sugar syrup. Move combs of brood to surround the queens, and place drawn, empty comb below the excluder for the queen to lay into. If you hold thirty queens in one bank valued at $20 per queen, it is certainly in your best interest to do this correctly. Otherwise you and your pocketbook will be pinched!

Keeping queens alive outside the hive—G.M. Doolittle carried queen cells in a box filled with cotton batting. I carried queens in cages (without attendants) in a small box with a tight lid, like a cigar box, furnished with a sponge holding water and provided with nurse bees shaken from a brood frame. I kept the box out of the sun and carried it with me, placing it in a safe, quiet place at night if I did not return to the queen bank. We caged old queens this way, and kept them on hand in case we had a nucleus that needed a queen until we could return with one.

Low acceptance of new queens

This is a list of factors that influence queen introduction and acceptance. Consider it a work in progress, since we are still learning how much we don't know about getting queens accepted into a colony.

1. Queen was released too quickly—There are clear biological processes that take time for queen introduction. If a queen is released within 72 hours after introduction into a new group of bees, I expect the worst. While you can use a toothpick or small nail to check to make sure the queen candy is not rock solid, don't stick it all the way through!
2. Queen was "immature"—While a virgin queen is able to mate and start laying eggs within 14 days, growing evidence shows higher acceptance when she is allowed to head up a mating nucleus or small colony for a full month before introduction. Very few queens get this treatment. Perhaps if they did beekeepers would have fewer queen problems.
3. Queen was damaged before introduction—If a queen is exposed to extreme heat or cold, dehydration or pesticides prior to installation, introduction success is unlikely. One Pennsylvania State University study showed huge temperature extremes in shipments of queens sent with temperature monitoring devices.
4. Queen was introduced into an unrelated stock—This is a problem experienced when you try to introduce a queen of one bloodline into a colony with little genetic overlap. I had trouble introducing Carniolian stock into Italian-mongrel bees. The only way we could get acceptance was to use bees containing some of the same Carniolian genetic material. This may be why some beekeepers have difficulty introducing Russian queens released by the USDA into their "American" bees.
5. The queen is sick or diseased—Queens with a midgut filled with parasites (Nosema), or exposed to heavy pesticide/miticide treatments, or weakened by starvation/dehydration are unlikely to be well-accepted.
6. The bees in the colony are too old or damaged—If old field bees are shaken from colonies after the honey crop with few nurse bees and given a queen, there is a decrease in the likelihood of queen acceptance. Bees damaged from pesticide or excessive miticide exposure may not have a healthy balance of young to old bees. However, a colony of primarily young bees will accept most queens.

7. Extreme robbing is underway—Hive-to-hive robbing draws many nurse and house bees away from their duties to defend the colony. Since any "foreign" bee is likely to be under attack, a new queen will be under attack as well. Use of a robbing screen will reduce this problem, but not eliminate it.
8. The colony is under nutritional stress—Hungry bees often turn against a new queen. If a colony has low stores and nothing coming in, it will set up stress-related behaviors that reduce queen acceptance. Feeding with sugar syrup helps increase acceptance levels.

Early supersedure

All of the conditions listed in the prior section may contribute to supersedure within two to six weeks after introduction. To this list we must add the following:
1. High mite or disease (Nosema) pressure on the colony.
2. Very poor weather conditions without supplemental feed.
3. "Nervous bees"—These are bees that build queen cells just in case the new management doesn't work out. Removal of queen cells often keeps the queen around for a normal life cycle.
4. Damaged queen—Workers detect queens that have been somehow damaged while instrumentally inseminated, clipped, marked or abused during natural mating and beekeeper shipping and handling. Many queens twist away while being clipped or marked and have a defective leg as a result. During either natural or instrumental mating there may be a blockage of the seminal fluids or mucus that plug the lateral or median oviduct, restricting or preventing her from laying normally. Queens that have been banked may have had their tarsi (foot pads) chewed by worker bees, and this reduces queen performance.
5. Queen failure without replacement supersedure by running out of sperm—When a queen runs out of sperm in the sperm storage organ in her abdomen, there does not appear to be a feedback mechanism that stops the queen from laying or stimulates the workers to replace her.

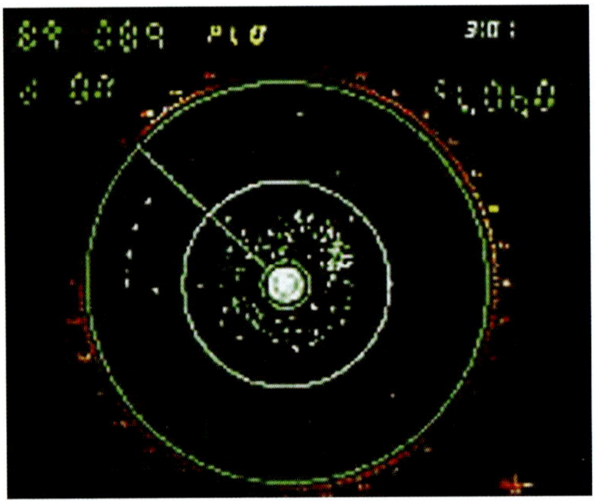

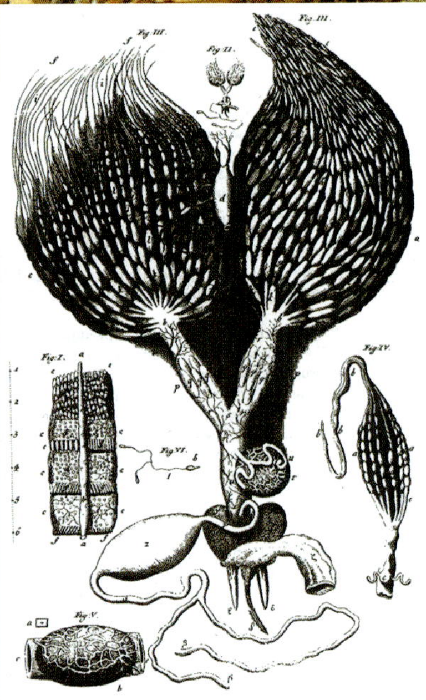

Previous page—Helium-filled balloons suspend a cage containing cotton soaked in queen pheromone. Taken to an drone congregation area or flyway, the pheromone attracts sexually mature drones already in the area. Mating occurs high in the sky, about 100 feet up, but the cage can be lowered to see the drone flight activity. Any beekeeper can duplicate this experiment and walk an area to determine where mating activity is taking place.
Top of page—Mature drones must have access to honey and pollen to develop and to refuel for mating flights. Poor honey reserves may cause worker bees to remove drones from the hive. Bottom left—Radar photo showing bee flight activity in a bee flyway to and from a mating area. USDA/Tucson. Bottom right—For successful mating, a queen must fill her oviduct (often called "rabbit ears" by inseminators) with sperm—5-8 million must migrate to the round spermatheca for full queen mating. File drawing.

III. The mating process

Drone congregation areas and flyways

Key to our understanding the mating of virgin queens and drones is our awareness of *drone congregation areas* (DCA's). Every afternoon—when the season and weather permit—sexually mature drones and virgin queens visit these permanent, aerial locations where they mate. There are no clear or specific geographic features humans may use to locate DCAs. Instead, we must find the mating bees themselves, starting along lines of trees and other naturally occurring features where bees might "pile up" during flight. Loper, Wolf and Taylor used modified radar to observe the nature of the DCAs and flyways.[16] DCAs are often 100 by 200 meters (328-656 feet) in size and reach into the sky 15 to 60 meters (50 to 200 feet) *Bee flyways* are lower areas 12-20 meters (39-66 feet) where bees travel to the DCAs. The flyways connects hives to the DCA and one DCA to another. The researchers found flyways to be up to 80 yards wide and up to two miles long; drones and queens have been observed to mate in these areas as well. They found 28 DCAs in a flyway network of routes used to cover the area. The locations are the same from year to year and are used for mating studies.

Drones gather in DCAs in the afternoon of a good flight day, rapidly flying about and out of the range of human vision, and using their large eyes (about twice the size of a worker's eyes and the largest of the bees) follow any virgin queen in the area. Older drones spend more time on mating flights than younger drones. However, the average length of life of a drone is 16-20 days after emergence from the cell. Almost all drones within 0.5 kilometer (0.3 miles) from a hive are between 8-10 days old.

Male bees do not respond to the queen in a colony, but in a DCA they respond to the odor produced by the queen's mandibular gland, the queen substance (*trans*-9-keto-2-decenoic acid and related components). The queen substance both attracts the drones and provides a strong sexual stimulation to mate; drones returning from a mating attempt are often so sexually charged that they often ejaculate with minimal touch.

---

[16]Loper, G.M., W.W. Wolf, and O.R. Taylor, Jr., 1992. Honey bee drone flyways and congregation areas, radar observations. *Kansas Entomological Society*, 65:223-230.

Green drone comb foundation placed on the edge of the brood nest.

In 1963 Cornell graduate student Norman Gary located DCAs by placing a queen or queen pheromone in a cage on a string attached to a weather balloon or kite, and moved around the fields and woods around Ithaca, New York, in an effort to find the areas where drones and queens were mating. The advantage of the balloon is it may be lowered to perhaps see some of the mating behavior, but this is relatively rare.

The balloon method has been modified into large drone traps that enabled researchers to collect, mark and release drones found within DCAs and to record their movement back to colonies and to other DCAs. One group of researchers collected non target drones (African drones) to kill them. On the following day they released drones from target colonies to obtain higher mating accuracy.

Most species of bees do not demonstrate this elaborate mating behavior. Queen and drone bumble bees will mate in a laboratory, and require no special address for sex. Nowhere but in the genus *Apis* do we observe males and queens that posses the unique combination of mating outside the hive and multiple males mating with virgin queens.

Distances covered by drones and queens

When H. Ruttner and F. Ruttner placed genetically marked virgin queens and three groups of genetically marked drones through a bee-free alpine valley, they found only a few matings occurred with drones from the vicinity of the queen's colony.[17] The average distance between apiary and mating location was more than 2 kilometers (.62 miles), and the maximum was 5 kilometers (1.55 miles). J. Woyke observed that queens had better mating success when drones were placed 2.5 kilometers (.77 miles) away from the apiary instead of being in the same location. Drones fly up to 3-6 kilometers (.9-1.8 miles) from the hive, and distances of 5 kilometers (1.5 miles) is common. The Ruttners estimate that drones from one location are able to fly over an area of 78 square kilometers (30 square miles). When Don Peer located mating nuclei at increasing distances from the drone source, using extreme isolation conditions, he obtained 89% mating at 5.7 kilometers (3.4 miles), 67% mating at 12.8 kilometers (8.0 miles) and 25% mating at 16 kilometers (10.0 miles) but only after 4 weeks.[18]

Drones have large thoraxic muscles, are nearly the same size as a queen, and are strong flyers. Yet, virgin queens fly further from the apiary than drones. The combined potential flight distance for drones and queens, and the large flight area of drones, reflect the tremendous difficulty of obtaining mating isolation in areas of intensive beekeeping or a healthy feral bee population. Even greater extremes are found in areas like deserts with limited bee populations, and do not represent typical behavior.

The mating flight

Queen maturation and flight

Prior to mating young queens leave the hive for short flights around the hive area. These are cleansing and orientation flights and not mating flights. Virgin queens leave the hive to mate anywhere between three and sixteen days after emergence. They only fly on days with fine weather—temperatures must be warmer than 20 degrees C. (68 degrees F.), and the wind must be relatively calm, under 10 mph. The majority of the queens mate between eight and twelve days, and, if mated, begin to lay eggs in the colony in ten to fourteen days. In queen production, queen mating units (mating nuclei) are usually checked at fourteen to twenty-one

[17]Ruttner, H., and F. Ruttner. 1972. Untersuchungen über die Flugaktivität und das Paarungsverhalten der Drohnen. 5. Drohnensammelplatz und Parungsdistanz. *Apidologie* 3: 203-232.

[18]Peer, D., 1957. Further studies on the mating range of the honeybee, *Apis mellifera. Can. Entomol.* 89:108-110.

days after mature cells are introduced to see if the young queen has emerged, mated and is laying successfully. Then the young queen is shipped to a customer or introduced into a production hive. The nucleus receives a ready-to emerge queen cell to repeat the mating process.

Drone maturation and flight

The spermatozoa in the drones testes migrate to the seminal vesicles when they are 3-8 days old and then require several days to mature. Drones start to make flights at the age of 4-14 days, flying between 1 p.m and 4 p.m standard time, the time changing seasonally according to photoperiod. Daily flight time is also influenced by variations in weather, climate, subspecies and flight activity the prior day.

During the initial mating flight the queen leaves the hive and travels by the network of flyways a mile or more to reach a mating area. Her brothers, however, use the flyways to reach the closest DCAs (drones within 0.5 kilometer (.16 miles) of the hive are young, 8-10 days of age). This means the virgin queen is in a mating area not populated with a large number of her youngest, sexually mature brothers. This minimizes inbreeding, and helps maintain vigorous colonies.

Some beekeepers check a mating colony to see if there are drones present for the queen to mate with in a DCA. Unfortunately, it really doesn't work that way; drones fly a shorter distance to a mating area and the virgin a greater distance. To establish and maintain some level of desired mating accuracy the beekeeper should check colonies producing target drones in the apiaries *surrounding* the mating yard; this will provide assurance that adequate drone numbers are present throughout the region. The area for large scale drone saturation should be on a radius of 2 miles (3.2 kilometer), or greater.

Mating behavior has been studied by several groups and from them we have obtained a few observations about the process. When a queen enters a DCA there are a large number of drones flying about, and her pheromones immediately attract their attention. Once in the area of the queen, the drones use their large eyes to orient to the queen (drones will chase objects the size and shape of queens if thrown into the mating area). As multiple drones are attracted to the queen, they form a *drone comet*, an arrangement of flying drones that are orienting to her scent plume. These comets may contain anywhere from a few to hundreds of drones, depending upon the local drone density.

When a drone reaches the queen, he touches the back of her abdomen and attempts to enter her sting chamber. Critical parts of the queen and drone align, and when the pheromones and when legs and key body parts are in the proper position, the queen opens her sting chamber, stimulating the drone's reproductive structure—the endophallus—to enter the queen. The drone is forced back violently by the strength of the hardening and compression of his abdominal and thoracic muscles. The drone separates from his endophallus left in the queen, falls to the ground and dies. Almost immediately another drone mounts the queen, the endophallus of the previous drone being forced out as he mounts her, repeating the process.

Orley Taylor reports that queens average 14 minutes for mating flights. If they fly one mile (1.6 kilometer) at 12 mph, they are able to fly out and back and have 4 minutes or more to mate with a quick succession of drones (O. Taylor, personal communication). Other researchers suggest that the mating flight runs 20-30 minutes, depending on the distance to the DCA.

After mating with up to 45 drones (average of 13.2) in one or more mating flights over one or more days, the queen returns to the hive where the worker bees remove the "mating sign", which is actually the remains of the endophallus from the last drone. The queen will groom herself and allow worker bees to lick and groom her body. This promotes selective sperm migration into the spermatheca from the mass of the average 87 million sperm held in her lateral oviducts. Since well-mated queens hold between 4 and 8 million sperm, the rest of the sperm are removed by the worker bees as thin strands of seminal material that rapidly dry and are carried out of the hive. All extra sperm are removed within 24 hours.

When the queen is prevented from getting a full allotment of sperm she will continue to fly on following days until she has reached the desired level of mating. It is not known what mechanism provides feedback that she has mated enough. It may be the number of drones, the volume of seminal fluid, hormonal changes, or some other trigger.

Once the mating process is completed, a queen will not return to the air to mate again. The only other time a queen will leave the have after mating is to fly with a swarm.

In 1792 F. Huber noted that if queens are prevented from leaving the hive until 21 days or more of age they became *drone layers*. This seems to be linked to age-related behavior.[19] Once mated the queen continues to lay eggs for the remainder of her life. A life expectancy of six months to three years is quite common, depending on highly variable conditions. Documented reports of queens that have lived five or more years persist in the literature. This is an exception for most beekeepers in the post-tracheal and varroa mite era of beekeeping.

Spermatheca

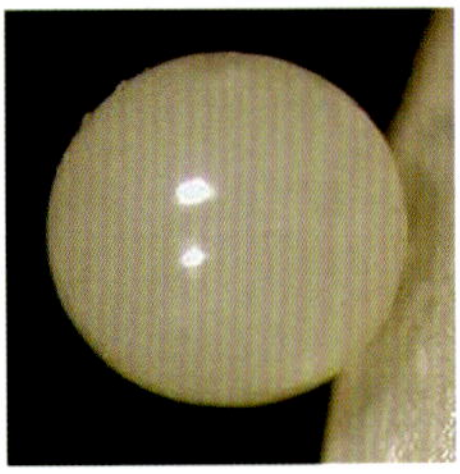

Spermatheca of undermated or queen running out of semen. USDA

The queen stores and maintains these foreign cells, the drone spermatozoa, in a structure called the spermatheca, located at the tip of the abdomen. Spermatozoa are kept under unique physiological conditions. The spermatheca is a fluid-filled sac made of chitin, the same material as the bee's exoskeleton, but very thin. This sac is surrounded by a layer of tracheal netting, all floating in the queen's blood, an energy rich environment of glucose, fructose, sucrose and trehalose. The movement of spermatozoa into the spermatheca is complicated, involving complex changes in the pH of the fluid and Na^+ and K^+ ions.

Mating risks

There are huge risks for outside mating. If the queen encounters a bird, dragonfly or some other predator, her colony's life is at risk. If she is unable to distinguish the entrance of her hive from that of the one next to it, she will undoubtedly be killed as she enters the wrong hive, and her colony will be left queenless. For a species to expose female reproductive bees to such potential harm suggests

[19] I instrumentally inseminated a few queens that were six weeks post emergence and they produced fertilized diploid daughters. However, I would sometimes have to remove an egg passing down the median oviduct to complete the insemination. One should assume that the amount of sperm migration was potentially restricted by eggs filling the lateral oviducts.

that mating in the open to a large potential pool of unrelated drones has enormous selective benefits. We will discuss in detail some of the proposed advantages to these behaviors in Section IV.

Drone saturation for mating

We just reviewed our knowledge of virgin queen and drone flight. Before the arrival of parasitic mites in the United States the population of bee colonies was more than twice what it is now. There were many feral (non-managed) colonies now largely absent from the environment. This has changed the population dynamics of reproductive sex in the quantity of drones available within the network of drone congregation areas.

How many drone colonies do you need?

The biggest question for those who raise queens is how many drone mother colonies—headed by queens of a particular genetic type, producing *target drones*—are needed to insure adequate queen mating. We will look at this in terms of timing (based on the calendar) and in numbers of drones needed.

In David Ives six-pack of one-act comedies titled *All in the Timing*, there is a very funny piece called *Words, Words, Words.* This shows three monkeys (played by grown men and women in monkey clothing) in a room filled with typewriters, all acting out the old adage that a room full of monkeys will eventually write *Hamlet* if given adequate time. It is a funny bit, reminding me of Rothenbuhler's room filled with queen propagators. There tends to be more screaming and yelling in the room filled with beekeepers than a room filled with monkeys when trying to determine the number of drones you need for a mating area for optimal mating.

When should I graft my queens?

Timing is everything in raising queens and getting them properly mated. The queen metamorphoses from egg to emerged adult in 15 to 17 days, the length depending on her race and growth environment. Drones metamorphose from egg to emergent adult in 24 to 25 days and are sexually mature in an average of 12 days with a reported range of 4 to 18 days. It is especially difficult to guarantee drone production early in the season when a colony's nutritional environment is substandard. The same is true in Florida and other locations during the summer, when very little nutrition is available to the colony.

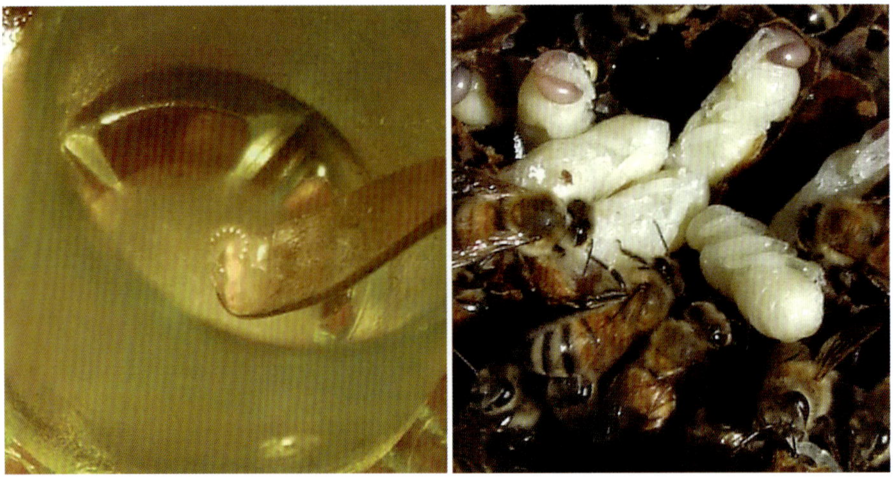

Timing of cell production is determined by production of abundant drones. When large numbers are sealed for five days (purple eyed stage), only then should cell production begin (grafting larva on left).

Both colony nutrition and the calendar must be checked to determine the ideal time to start queen cell production. The optimal age coordination for queen cell starting (grafting) is when drone brood has been sealed brood stage for five days. Since it is nearly impossible to tell how long brood has been sealed, beekeepers should uncap cells and graft only when they see purple-eyed or older brood.

This takes in account the different developmental rates of queens and drones, including their different rates of reaching sexual maturity. It is our best prediction of when both vigorous, sexually mature drones and virgin queens may meet in a drone congregation area. Some queens develop faster, and some drones will develop slower. As a result you are strongly advised to keep records of your own observations and adjust for your local environmental conditions and bee stocks.

These are biological events, subject errors. We normally assume that queen eggs will take 15-16 days from oviposition to virgin emergence, knowing some strains develop in less time. There is also the human factor—if a beekeeper transfers a larvae that is older than 24 hours into a queen grafting cup, the resulting queen will emerge earlier because she was already older to start with.

Exceptions abound. Some beekeepers and breeders maintain that drones are sexually ready to mate 4-8 days after emergence. I advise considerable caution here: drones make orientation and cleansing flights at this age, but that does not mean that they are ready for sex! These drones taking orientation flights may not have completed sperm migration and maturation.

How many sealed drone brood cells do I need?

I recommend you *estimate* the amount of drone brood in production in *square inches of sealed drone brood*. For example, a drone comb with an area of sealed drone brood ten inches wide by five inches tall, represents fifty square inches of sealed drone brood. If drones are in production on both sides of the comb, double that for one hundred square inches of sealed drone brood. Since there are *about* four drone cells per inch, *one square inch of sealed drone brood represents about sixteen drones*. In this comb, there are *as many as* 1,600 drones in development (16 drones x 100 sq inches). While you might count the exact number of developing drones, it is easier to *estimate* the number of square inches of drone brood as you work. If a colony produces 5,000 drones in one season, this one comb represents nearly one third of its annual drone production. But if a colony produces 20,000 drones in one season, this comb represents just eight percent of the annual production. Differences in the vigor, strength, and genetic influences contribute to the variation you will see from colony to colony.

Start out with a ruler and measure a few frames and do the math. You will soon train your eye to estimate the amount of sealed drone cells in the colony. Record this information—it is a human estimate of a biological process that will probably change if the physiology of the hive changes or if you have chalkbrood, since both will reduce the amount of brood on that comb.

Sealed drone brood represents the drone egg laying of the queen for 14 days, reduced by the number of eggs and larvae consumed by the worker bees as they trim brood as part of drone physiology, and losses due to disease. All colonies experience some drone trimming. There is less during the spring buildup period and more in the summer and fall. However, if you divide the number of sealed drone brood cells by fourteen, you have an estimate of the daily production of drones by this colony at this point in time. The rate of drone production will be different on April 15, May 15, June 15 and so on throughout the year due to all the complicated factors involved in drone production.

When we divide our comb of 1,600 sealed drone cells by 14 we have an average[20] of 114 new drones produced each day. That is the *maximum* number of new drones added to the supply that will be available for mating when mature. This is not an adequate supply of drones when you are attempting to mate dozens, hundreds or thousands of queens.

Studies have shown that drones only live 16 to 20 days after emerging. If a drone matures and takes his first mating flight at 12 days, but dies on his 20th day, he has just one week of potential mating activity! Ironically, about 96% of all drones do not mate, but die. That means that there may not be as many drones in the drone congregation areas as we might think. There is attrition in the number of drones due to disease (chalkbrood and others), parasitic mites, neglect by worker bees, bird and insect predation, accidents, and chemical contamination by beekeepers. Weather interferes with food supplies that may stimulate worker cannibalism and destruction of drone brood even in the sealed cell stage. Cold weather and miticides may interfere with sperm migration so not all the adult drones will provide sperm for the queen if they mate with her.

In an aggressive queen mating environment, the percentage of drones that mate must be higher than 4%. Commercial beekeepers using queen cells to make nucleus colonies for increase, and a queen propagation firm attempting to produce 500, 1000 or more mated queens per week require huge drone numbers. When mating is finished in these operations, the drone producing colonies should still have abundant drones. If they do not, then even the weakest, sickest and least desirable drones have successfully passed on their genes to your new colonies. You seek competition of vigorous drones in the mating area (and not from African bees or neighbor colonies). Highly saturated mating areas provide the only known method of maintaining this competition.

Estimating the amount of drone brood required per queen

It is very useful to compute the square inches of sealed drone

[20]Drone oviposition by the queen is undoubtedly quite uneven, especially in the early spring with fluctuating environmental conditions, so daily average is highly variable it helps understand drone rearing dynamics.

brood needed to supply the number of drones required for mating, and doing so on a *per queen* basis. This predicts the density and completion level in the DCAs. It must allow for loss of drone numbers throughout the developmental path of the bees, and allocate a certain number of drones that will not mate with the queen, but may provide competition for non-target drones, such as African drones.

Two square inches of drone brood per queen cell—This level of drone production reflects the conditions found in many parts of the United States and Canada prior to the arrival of parasitic mites and African bees. In the early 1980s there were twice as many beekeepers managing three to four times the number of colonies. There were also uncounted feral colonies in bee trees and the sides of buildings contributing to drone abundance in the former scheme of colony mating. The drones and virgin queens were not subjected to harsh chemicals to control mites, chemicals that have been shown to reduce the number, viability, sperm count and general health of available drones.

Four square inches of drone brood per queen cell—This describes our current situation, with far fewer beekeepers, fewer viable colonies, more colonies in flux due to mite attacks, very low numbers of feral colonies, and lower drone production per hive. While there are areas of traditional drone saturation where migratory and commercial beekeepers operate, the colonies have likely been medicated with miticides (such as coumophos), and the number of viable drones is reduced. Beekeepers experience poor queen mating, more failure of new queens in packages and increase hives, and much shorter queen and hive survival.

Eight square inches of drone brood per queen cell—This environment contains many unwanted drones, perhaps African, that may be more competitive than managed drones (genetically or not chemically addled) and where accuracy in mating is very important. In this mating arena there are few managed colonies in the area producing target or at least beneficial drones. There are, however, a larger number of colonies that you do NOT want your virgin queens to mate with.

These examples produce surplus drones so there are abundant drones and they have a good chance at resulting in *at least 50%*

accurate mating. This minimal level seems to be very critical. Fifty percent mating accuracy was what we wanted queen cooperators to achieve when we ran the Starline and Midnite programs—with less too much of the hybrid benefit was lost. Marla Spivak, one of the developers of the Minnesota Hygienic line of bees, indicated that in order to obtain hygienic behavior, at least half of the drones needed to be hygienic drones, carrying these desired traits. If less than 50% of the drones a queen mates with are not hygienic, the colony does NOT demonstrate expected hygienic traits. A similar comment has been published about the USDA-released Russian stock—when there are 50% or more Russian drones involved in the cross, the level of varroa resistance is adequate to make an impact on colony health.

So, what number of colonies do you need to obtain a minimum 50% accurate mating to target drones? Here are some key points:

1. *Number of drones that mate with a queen.* David Tarpy has reviewed the research and presented evidence that single virgin queen will mate with up to 45 drones—the average was 13.2 drones (See Section IV). Looking at his distribution data there was a significant number of virgins that mated with up to 20 drones. This suggests that to be on the safe side, or to increase mating accuracy, we should expect to have each virgin mate with 20 drones. This helps insure that the healthiest and most competitive drones successfully mate with the virgins.

2. *How many drones can a drone mother colony produce?* There is enormous variation in the drone production from different colonies beekeepers may selected for this purpose. If we use a 10 inch by 5 inch comb with drone brood on both sides, that gives us 100 square inches of sealed drone cells, for an average of 7.1 square inches of drone brood *per day* during the buildup and swarming season. Remember drone brood is sealed for 14 days, so divide the number of square inches of sealed drone brood by 14 to get an *estimate* of the colony's average drone production.

3. *How many drone combs will a colony fill?* Some northern state beekeepers have colonies that will produce 2 or 3 large drone combs during May and early June and then cut back to less than one full frame of drones in late June and July. The overall drone population changes colony drone production, as does the nectar

flow. Since drones are reported to live an average of just 20 days, we will take a conservative approach, and estimate that the average colony will produce just one frame of sealed drone brood—on average—throughout a season (half a year or 26 weeks) or less than 3000 drones. This is well below the reported production of 5000 to 20,000 drones per season mentioned elsewhere. Yet this allows for reduced production, drone cannibalism, chemical damage and poor beekeeping conditions. Our objective is to produce adequate drone numbers and not to run short.

Finally, the number of queens you plan to mate each day will determine the number of drones needed in your mating area. For example, if you plan to run 100 queen cells into nuclei colonies every day during the mating season[21], you will need about 14 colonies to produce drones if you are in the "historic" situation described above. For the "current" level of fewer surrounding drones, you need to double that to 28 colonies to supply the necessary drones. However, if you are in an area of highly "competitive" drone production, you should consider supplying 56 colonies within the mating yards to do nothing but raise drones.

The drone producing colonies should not be in one location, but spread out within a two mile radius around the mating area to insure that the far flying queens meet up with the drones you produced just for her.

Drone holding colonies

Drone comb, natural, plastic or modified comb

Beekeepers usually already own the equipment needed to produce special colonies dedicated to the holding—and feeding—of a larger number of developing and flying target drones. These colonies are like full sized nucleus colonies, made up in out-yards where target drones are being produced in a number of colonies. Both worker and drone brood is harvested from these colonies and combined into drone holding units. Since drone brood is sealed for 14 days, this plan works well when based on a two week work schedule. If you fall behind a few days, you still have time to insure a good drone harvest. Here are the key parts of this system.

[21]This is a large mating operation. If you install 100 queen cells every day, you will operate 1400 mating nuclei if you pull queens every 14 days, 1700 nuclei if you pull queens every 17 days, and a whopping 2100 nuclei if you plan to harvest queens every three weeks.

Drone brood produced during the almond bloom in February and early March in California.

Target drone mother—Every colony producing drones for use in the mating area must be headed by a target drone mother—one that produces the drones you want to mate with the queen. Target drone mothers may all be from the same line, or a mixture of queens of different lines that you have purchased or raised that possess characteristics you seek in your final production colonies. If you are using a line-breeding plan, target drone mothers are the best colonies in your operation NOT used as grafting stock.

Working the colonies on a 14-day schedule it is unlikely you will miss any queen superseded—you noticing queen cells and other changes involved in queen replacement. This means that you need only see the queen at the start of the cycle and at random times during the season. Keep notes to insure the maintenance of these important queens, just to make sure. If you have any doubt about the queen producing drones in a colony, do not use them in the breeding program.

Push drone brood production—Early and increased drone production is achieved by locating the apiaries where there is excellent late winter and spring buildup—plenty willow, maple and other plants that contribute a strong pollen flow. Nectar flows help, but all colonies should be fed a 1:1 sucrose syrup in case the nectar fails. Add one or two frames of emerging worker brood from non-target colonies to each drone mother colony to boost the strength of the colony and obtain early production of target drones.

Drone combs—Dadant and Sons has offered drone cell wax foundation for many years. The Pierco Company makes a plastic drone foundation that is green in color. The color makes it easier to find the combs and check them. Some beekeepers use a partial frame with worker cells above and drone cells below (or leave an open space for the bees to fill with drone brood). Early in the season use only drawn combs, but at season's peak you may find you can use drone foundation efficiently.

Drone combs are placed at the edge of the brood nest, between the last frame of worker brood and the frame containing pollen. Since drones must be in production at the five-day sealed stage when a queen is started (grafting), drone combs must be placed in the colony no later than 18-24 days before you start grafting, allowing the bees time to work the comb and contemplate drone production.

Some queen propagators put three drone combs to drone mother colonies, one comb every 10 days. Their intent is to keep drones in production at all ages during the mating season. This system of drone holders works best with either one or two drone combs per drone mother colony.

Harvesting drone combs—When a drone frame contains primarily sealed drone cells, it may be moved to a special *drone holding colony*. Like making a nucleus, you assemble the colony from a number of colonies by removing frames of sealed drone brood, as well as frames of sealed worker brood along with the nurse bees on these combs. Add one or two frames of stored honey and pollen to the outside of the nest. If you keep nine frames in a ten-frame deep hive body, the arrangement of the combs may look like this:

H/P-W-D-W-D-W-D-W-H/P

In this arrangement the H/P represents a frame holding honey and pollen, the W is a frame of sealed worker brood, and the D is a frame of sealed drone brood. If there do not seem to be adequate nurse bees on the combs, shake frames of bees from the brood nest, inspecting first to make sure the queen is not on the comb. While this drone holding colony holds three drone brood frames, a fourth frame my be added, perhaps by removing one of the H/P frames. If your holding colony has 3 frames of 1600 drones in development, you may have a total of 4800 drones emerging and available for mating in the yard. If you have 4 frames you may have as many as 6400 drones at your service.

This drone-holding (and feeding) colony should be either moved to the mating area or to a holding location where the drones may emerge and mature. But make sure they are in the mating area by the time they are sexually mature.

Since the colony is essentially a large nucleus colony filled with a large population of young workers, we block off part of the entrance of the colony to reduce robbing by other colonies. We placed a *newly emerged virgin queen in a secure cage* and placed the cage between two brood frames. Because she is a virgin queen, and cannot mate, she provides a key feature of these drone-holding colonies—to duplicate the conditions of a colony undergoing queen replacement, where drones will be cared for well. Place containers of thin sugar syrup in an empty shell over the brood nest. This serves as a stimulus to the worker bees, and keeps the workers and the drones well fed. Since drones may fall into a division board or frame feeder and die, do not use them.

If you made this unit up 14 days after the drone frames were put into the colony, and there was predominately sealed drone cells on the combs, these drones will emerge in 10 more days, and will require up to 12 days to reach sexual maturity before they will be able to mate. If you mark you calendar that the drones should be emerged and making mating attempts three weeks after the colonies you will have an easy record keeping chore.

If the drones produced from these colonies were all in the sealed brood stage, and if you made them up 14 days after the drone comb went into the hive, the drones will be very close in age, about four days. This means that the drone holding colonies will be producing young vigorous drones for about one week, when they will start to die. At that point we removed the caged virgin queen and introduce a mated queen. The drone combs are removed and the colony becomes an increase colony, perhaps adding a super if the nectar flow is underway.

Varroa control for drone holding colonies

We have potential conflict when we leave drone comb in colonies. Varroa mites prefer drone brood because of their longer reproductive cycle, so there is a chance drone comb moved from the drone mother colonies may have varroa mites on them. So, we need to keep a few facts in mind:

1. Use mite-resistant stock for target drone colonies, so the number of varroa mites in the drone cells should be lower than in non-resistant colonies.

2. Drone holding colonies are ideal for IPM-type management. I suggest the use of screened bottom boards and powdered sugar dusting if there appear to be a large number of mites in the colony. Since these colonies are used just once, there is no opportunity for the varroa mites to build up beyond he number of drones already present. Before the colony is turned over as an increase colony, treat it with one of the so-called natural miticides to knock down the number of mites remaining in the colony if you feel it is necessary.

Eliminating non-target drones by trapping and chemical use

Another idea for the control of unwanted drones is to adapt a program of eliminating non-target drones from your apiary. There are several possible methods to suggest:

1. Use drone comb in all non-target colonies and remove the sealed drone brood and destroy it by freezing it or cutting it out with a large scraper (if using plastic foundation).

2. During morning hive workup when drones do not normally fly, install queen excluders on the *bottom* of colonies of non-target drones to prevent their flight. DO NOT use a piece of queen excluder material at the entrance of the hive, since hundreds of sexually mature drones WILL block the entrance and cause the colony to *overheat* and will KILL THE COLONY. Use this method to control drones in your neighbor's colonies if you have their permission. Perhaps a free mite-resistant queen, installed at no charge, will earn their support.

3. Using modified flight traps in DCAs, non-target drones have been trapped and killed, removing them from the competition for target drones.

Producing off-season drones in Florida

On October 31, 1979 several of my associates at Genetic Systems Inc. and I established an investigation to see if we could stimulate drone production before the date of normal drone rearing.

We grouped equalized colonies in threes and installed instrumentally inseminated Starline queens (HG x aEF) of the same age and HG grafting mother. We kept additional sister queens in the same apiary for replacement if a queen failed during the experiment. Queens were installed with push-in cages on November 7 and 8.

Each colony consisted of an empty deep hive body with a bottom board containing a sixty-watt electric light bulb. The socket was fastened to one side of the hive body. Above the empty hive body was double screen with an entrance for bee flight. Above that were two deep brood chambers containing bees and comb. The top chamber also contained a division board feeder that was kept filled with 1:1 syrup as a means of stimulation and to counteract any drying effect from the light. We also fed the Dadant and Sons, Inc. protein product Quickgro, which contained no natural pollen. The substitute was placed immediately over the brood area of each colony.

Colonies had full flight and collected pollen and nectar on good flight days. On November 12, 1979 we started two treatments and a control. The first treatment was set on a time clock so all the colonies (one in each group of three) had the light bulb on for 18 hours and off for 6. We called this the long day treatment.

The second was the increasing day treatment. We started at the day length of 11/12/79 of 11 hrs and 18 minutes when the light bulb was on. We increased the day length 10 minutes each day, alternating between morning and afternoon (at both ends of the light period). Lights were on during the daylight hours.

The control group colonies were established in the same manner as the treatment groups, but did not have a light bulb.

Data collection—We measured the amount of worker and drone brood produced in each colony by estimating the brood frame equivalent (BFE) for each colony. Simply put, we scored each frame with a fraction of brood to the nearest tenth, and added the number to obtain the amount of brood present. We made observations on 11/15 and 12/12 1979 and 1/7 and 2/12 1980. An additional drone brood count was taken 1/18 1980.

The worker brood observations showed a slight increase in the increasing day colonies on the 12/12 inspection, but the greatest difference was on 1/7 and 2/12, when the long day treatment had one more BFE than the control colonies.

Drone brood production started in the two treatments on 1/7 but not until 2/12 for the control, over a month earlier. On 1/7, 1/18 and 2/12, the long day treatment had .19 BFE compared to 2.9 BFE in the increasing day treatment. These positions switched, so that b y 2/12 the long day treatment had produced a sum of .94 BFE while the increasing day treatment had produced a sum of .82 BFE of drone comb. The control had .4 BFE on 2/12.

In terms of viable drones for inseminations, we see the most dramatic differences. The control group drones were used to inseminate 133 virgin queens, the increasing day length drones inseminated 273 virgins and the long day group inseminated 306 virgins. Each queen received 8 microliters of semen. We were able to harvest mature drones from the two treatment groups a full month earlier than the control group.

Our little experiment played with both light and heat, but provided a low cost method to get valuable drones a full month earlier than Nature. In a breeding program, these early queens may have saved a line or met the needs of queen propagators who needed grafting stock for their spring production. In 1980 dollars, I valued the benefit of the drones produced from this experiment at $5,000. If I extrapolated these queens into $100 breeder queens in today's market, we could easily have exceeded the potential production of over one half million dollars worth of stock.

We can produce mid-winter drones and use them to inseminate virgins. An ordinary light bulb is a powerful stimulant to a colony's brood rearing cycle, coordinating it with an increasing day or long day light application. While this may seem like a great deal of bother to the ordinary beekeeper, to the serious queen breeder with important stock to produce, the light bulb may help accelerate the production of viable queens.[22]

It would be interesting to use a modification of this method to produce large number of drones early in the season and attempt

[22]For a complete report of this study, review L Connor, 2004. Stimulating drone development during winter in Florida. *Bee Culture.* 132:27-29

to mate virgin queens naturally before other colonies have mature drones. Such a temporal mating shift has unexplored potential for the commercial queen breeder. It may be risky, but worth the effort.

Right—Varroa mite on adult bee. USDA-CCD. Below—deformed wing and K-wing affected worker bees. Both are caused by viruses associated with varroa mites.

IV. Colony genetics

Sex determination

Various methods exist for creating male and female individuals. In humans, the chromosome for sex determination is X in the egg and either X or Y in the sperm. Individuals who are XX (one X on each chromosome) are female, and those who are XY (with X on one and Y on the other chromosome) are male.

Other animals use a different system for sex determination. It is estimated that about twenty percent of animals are *haplodiploid*—fertilized diploid (two sets of chromosomes, for a total of 32) develop into females, while haploid individuals (one set of chromosomes for a total of 16) develop into males.

When we study the gene involved in sex determination in the wasps, sawflies, ants and bees, we find that the *sex of an individual is determined if there is one allele or two different alleles for the sex determination gene*. The gene found in honey bees produces an arginine serine-rich protein type. With two different alleles that generate the protein, a female develops. If there is one or two of the same alleles, only one protein is produced and a male develops.

Fertilized (diploid) eggs in honey bees are usually female because they have two different alleles, and thus two different proteins. But when the same allele appears at the sex determination gene, producing the same protein, then the individual is a male, what we call a *diploid male*. These diploid drones are produced in all bee colonies at differing frequencies. When the egg of a diploid drone hatches it produces an odor that stimulates the worker nurse bees to eat the young larva within a few hours. This effectively prohibits the production of two different drone types.[23]

The number of sex alleles in a population of bees varies considerably. There may be 16 to 20 different sex alleles, leading to many sex allele combinations and a high degree of haploid drone production. But when stocks are closely related, as with line breeding programs where genes are concentrated for potential hybridiza-

[23]Diploid drones have been produced in the laboratory and studied. For a review of this work, consult Woyke, J., 1969. A method of rearing diploid drones in a honeybee colony. *J. Apic. Res.* 8:65-74.

Frame of worker brood showing missed cells due to the combination of the same allele for sex determination from both the queen and the drone. Instead of developing as a diploid female, it develops as a diploid drone. Soon after hatching, the young larvae trigger a feeding response to remove them from the brood comb, resulting in the missing cells.

tion, there may be only two alleles for sex, and the brood pattern will be half workers and half diploid drones, which are quickly removed by the workers. While this is an unacceptable brood pattern because with fifty percent brood viability a colony is unable to increase worker bee numbers, it also shows what the theory looks like in nature. This sort of brood pattern is often called *shot gun* brood.

Most colonies have a number of sex alleles and the level of drone brood production is usually under five percent of the fertilized eggs. When a stock has been isolated in geography, as in an island system, the level of inbreeding will be greater than ten percent.

All beekeepers must monitor the appearance of the brood pattern in a hive. If there is considerable spotty brood (shotgun brood), this is a strong evidence of inbreeding. Be careful in evaluating newly established hives and queens. In colonies with queens that pass on hygienic behavior to their worker daughters, the shotgun appearance may be reflected the worker's cell cleaning effort to eliminate mites or disease. Look at the uncapped brood to determine if inbreeding (spotty brood in the larval stage) or hygienics (not spotty at the larval stage) is involved.

Bee disease, bee sex and "curiously promiscuous" queens

Most beekeepers quickly become familiar with bee diseases—chalkbrood, sacbrood, and the foulbroods—European and American. They learn there are more, especially the viruses associated with parasitic mites. Viruses and mites (or is it mites and viruses) provide a "one-two" punch for a lot of beehives and their owners. Often beekeepers think that the key to disease control it to keep a colony "healthy." But how do you achieve that healthy state? Do you avoid contact with all other colonies (good luck), keep your bees confined to certain foraging areas (please, please tell me just how do you plan to do that?), and keep them well fed and growing? Perhaps you were taught that having disease in your hives meant that you were a bad beekeeper. Many of us act that way by hiding diseased colonies. But the truth is that most bee diseases are picked up by colonies as a function of local geography—exposure to dead and dying hives, migrations of mite-infected bees from these dying hives, a season that favors disease development and the bees' inability to deal with diseases when kept in multi-colony apiaries. Allowing disease to remain in managed colonies, in my opinion, is the part that should be considered unacceptable.

You might be surprised to learn that researchers have been looking at the relationship between disease (in all organisms as well as bees) and how they are responsible for two remarkable biological events: the development of sex (male-female exchange of genetic materials) and the evolutionary pressure for the development of queens that mate with more than one drone.

The Red Queen and the evolution of sex

Lets examine these evolutionary concepts one at a time. We will discuss the *development of sex* first. In evolutionary biology there is the concept that sex evolved to overcome the constant pressure from disease, for a constant genetic recombination of genes, and, the theory argues, is the best method to stay one step ahead of diseases, pests and parasites. This concept was described in a book by English science writer Matt Ridley, titled *The Red Queen: Sex and the Evolution of Human Nature*. The *Red Queen* in question here is not a bee or even an insect; but refers to the Red Queen chess piece in Lewis Carroll's *Through the Looking-Glass* that runs frantically yet remains stationary. Ridley explains how the metaphor of the Red Queen describes the nature of the genetic relationship between host and disease. It has been studied in humans and recently examined in honey bees. The Red Queen's speeding race that gets her nowhere puts reproductive sex in the center of the evolutionary spotlight. Not without controversy, this concept has important lessons beekeepers must apply to honey bee queens of many colors installed into our white and multicolored beehives.

Social insects occupy nests that are crowded and humid, the perfect conditions and highly favorable environment promoting the growth of pathogens and the rapid transmission of diseases from individual to individual. Social insects have evolved elaborate and complicated behaviors that help manage diseases under these conditions. An example is found in certain leaf-cutting ants, where one caste of tiny farmer ants constantly monitors the fungi growing on the leaf pieces. These ants are small and quick enough to remove sections of a harmful fungus whenever it appears in the leaf farms of the colony. This allows the ants to grow without contamination only the species or strain of fungus that they use for food. These tiny ants react much faster than human farmers who rarely note any disease or pest problem until it has become widespread and difficult to control.

In honey bees, of course, we have discovered the process of hygienic behavior, where bees somehow detect defective brood cells—infected cells producing an odor cue that stimulates the bees to remove the cell's contents. Remarkably, this same genetic mechanism has been shown to successfully work on a number of very different, highly unrelated diseases and even mites: American foulbrood, chalkbrood, virus-killed brood, chilled brood, and, of course, varroa mites. All are managed using the same basic bad cell odor detection and cell cleaning mechanism. The Minnesota hygienic, SMR/VSR, Russian and other bee lines demonstrate some variation or even the identical genetic hygienic mechanism as outlined by Professor Walter Rothenbuhler in the mid 1950s.

Advantages of multiple mating

If we accept the idea that the best way to distribute adaptive genetic mutations and changes protective to the genome of a species is through sex, we are still faced with an explanation for why bees of the genus *Apis* have evolved the behavior of mating multiple times and using drone congregation areas (DCA's) where queens mate with a dozen or more drones within a short time interval. What is the advantage of one queen mating with so many drones?

Most insects mate only once, and within the social insects the only reports of multiple mating have been in *Vespula* (yellow jacket wasps), *Atta* (leaf-cutter ants), *Pogonomyrmex* (harvester ants), and *Dorylus* and *Eciton* (army ants). But the social insects with the highest level of multiple mating are all in the genus *Apis*, with queens of *Apis mellifera* mating with 13 drones on average as based on molecular genotyping.

North Carolina State University researcher David Tarpy and Cornell scientist Tom Seeley have worked with queens mated to different numbers of drones and examined their ability to counteract disease. We will review some of their work to examine the role of multiple mating in the overall success of the honey bee.

Tarpy and Seeley studied the "curious promiscuity" of queen bees and how the queen's multiple mating behavior impacts the beehive. There must be a huge evolutionary payback for a species to invest in the complicated mating system found in the honey bee species. Rather than mating in or around the nest, virgin honey bee queens and drones fly to drone congregation areas (DCAs) to mate. On their flight they are exposed to predators, high winds, sudden changes in the weather, and may make orientation mistakes returning to the proper hive. Why does a queen mate multiple times and then stop for the rest of her life?

Sex and the single queen

To answer this question, I reviewed two related papers. The first is by David Tarpy and compares queens that have been instrumentally inseminated with either one drone (SDI) or with many drones (MDI)[24] In the second paper, Tarpy worked with Cornell's Tom Seeley (where Tarpy had worked as a post-doc before being hired by NCSU) and they conducted a similar study to evaluate different colonies[25]. In each paper they produced two groups of colonies. One group consisted of highly related virgin queens that were instrumentally mated with the semen of just one drone, each

[24]Tarpy, D.R. 2002. Genetic diversity within honeybee colonies prevents severe infections and promotes colony growth. *Proc. R. Soc. London B* 270: 99-103

[25]Tarpy, D.R and T.D. Seeley. 2006. Lower disease infections in honeybee (*Apis mellifera*) colonies headed by polyandrous vs monandrous queens. *Naturwissenschften*, 93: 195-199.

drone taken from an unrelated colony. The second group of queens was instrumentally mated with an identical volume of semen collected from unrelated drones—one each from the colonies used in the first group. After the semen was collected and mixed, one micro-liter of semen was given to each queen. This is the same amount of semen given to each queen mated to one drone. This second group of queens were mated in such a way as to duplicate the number of drones the average queen mates with in the wild, but under highly controlled conditions. Once established in production hives, the colonies were examined for disease and general aspects of beekeeping. The two groups of colonies allowed the researchers to compare colonies mated to one drone, called *monandrous colonies,* where the worker bees were genetically similar; to colonies mated with multiple drones, called *polyandrous colonies*, and where the resulting colonies had genetically diverse worker bees. The experiment allowed them to examine any possible advantage of polyandry.

Colonies were set up and managed for six weeks so they had worker bees from the queen. At that time, each colony was inoculated with spores of chalkbrood fed in pollen patties. Infected brood was counted and compared between the two groups.

The results showed that the colonies with a diverse number of drones had a lower *variation* in disease development when compared to the colonies with a queen mated to a single drone. Tarpy concluded that genetically diverse colonies (polyandrous) may be better able to prevent severe infections of chalkbrood because they reduced the variability found in the occurrence of disease. These colonies did express some chalkbrood, but not at the extremely high or the extremely low levels found in the monandrous colonies. Genetic variation has been shown to exist in bee populations for most bee diseases and mites, including chalkbrood, *Varroa destructor, Acarapis woodi, Nosema apis,* and American foulbrood. Tarpy's study indicated that polyandrous colonies were less likely to experience a severe chalkbrood infestation. He wrote *"that increased genetic diversity within colonies provides them with several benefits, and thus should be viewed as a trait with pluralistic consequences."*

Lower disease infections with multiple mating

In the second study Tarpy conducted in cooperation with Tom

Parasitic mite syndrome (PMS) showing European foulbrood like symptoms and sunken cappings. Associated with deformed wings and small bee size.

Seeley, various techniques were refined, so while the methods used in the two experiments were not identical they were very similar. Again single-drone inseminated queens were produced and compared to multiple-drone inseminated queens and their resulting colonies. In the second study, the colonies were exposed to natural conditions and evaluated for the presence and frequency of bee diseases. Of the 20 final colonies, 80% had one or more of four diseases: sacbrood, chalkbrood, European foulbrood or American foulbrood. Of these, the MDI colonies had less variability in both chalkbrood and in all disease combined. Colonies headed by MDI queen had significantly more comb and more frames of brood.

These results show that with increased genetic diversity multiply inseminated queen colonies may produce subgroups (sometimes called *super sisters*) of worker bees with unique behavioral skill sets. It is thought these subgroups may specialize in certain chores, like finding food resources or maintaining a more uniform brood nest temperature. Second, the multiple drone mating reduces the chance of having the same allele for the sex gene, and reduces the amount of missed brood due to diploid drone removal. Third, the increased diversity of the colony may mean that colonies are more likely to moderate the levels of diseases and parasites in the colonies.

Of these three ideas, this research supports the third concept, of reduced disease. But the study does not contradict the first two concepts, for “the genetically more diverse colonies may have benefited in multiple ways.”

The ecology of honey bee colonies is significantly affected by disease—colonies started as swarms on new equipment showed four brood pathogens in less than two months. It reflects the overwhelming role of disease in colonies life. The test colonies were kept in pairs and were widely separated and not manipulated during the experiment to prevent cross-contamination.

Lessons for beekeepers

From 1976-1980 I worked with the old Starline/Midnite technology of creating inbred lines to cross via instrumental insemination to create hybrid bees, and was trained to develop many genetically uniform hives. Queens were very closely related including the drone producers. The key was to develop highly uniform bees, demonstrating hybrid vigor and physically larger bees that were more productive. The goal was to produce hybrid colonies that all required the same management at the same time—every hive gets two supers today—sort of thinking. The diseases that were our primary concerns were the two foulbroods, a little sacbrood, the newly introduced chalkbrood, and silent battles with *Nosema apis*. Many beekeepers used drugs (we were likely to call them medications) on a regular basis.

The hybrid bees had little tolerance against either the tracheal or varroa mites. Nationally we have lost a lot of colonies, and a great deal of genetic diversity. We certainly lost a huge number of very uniform, highly productive stocks.

We did not talk about diversity except to test new queens for possible integration into the hybrid program. Many queen lines were evaluated but precious few were integrated; the queens that failed to make the cut were pinched off and the stock rejected from the program.

Now beekeepers are looking at ways to increase diversity in the bees. The work of Tom Seeley and David Tarpy shows the advantage in having a large number of unrelated drones mate with queens and thus provide a mechanism to reduce the extreme cases of disease. Over the next decade I hope that individual beekeepers, as well as new bee breeding groups will identify certain genetic strengths in their stocks, and include such stocks in a drone saturation plan to increase the genetic diversity of the drones in drone congregation areas.

At the end of Tarpy and Seeley's second paper, the authors wrote: *"The curiously high promiscuity of honey bee queen is an adaptation to minimize the impact of the litany of parasites that threaten their colonies, More generally, the findings of this study, together with the many studies supporting the Red Queen hypothesis for the evolution of sexual reproduction, suggest that disease is a fundamentally important agent in natural selection and that genetic diversity plays a key role in minimizing fitness losses imposed by disease."*

Superfamilies, super-sisters, hive control and decision making

Another fascinating aspect of recent honey bee biological research has been attempts to integrate the role of the multiple drone mating with concepts of colony control and decision making within the colony. Because worker bees in a colony have one mother and many fathers, sister workers of the hive are not identical. Instead they form various sub-families of sister workers that share a particular father. These are called *super-sisters*, and the entire colony of these different super-sisters make up the *super-family* that we call the bee colony.

It has been shown that individual worker bees belonging to the same sub-family are able to recognize each other and distinguish their super-sisters from their half-sisters. This has led some researchers to test to see if there may be some effort by these super-sisters to promote their special interests and increase the reproductive fitness of their particular subfamily. However, any potential nepotism must be mediated by the evolutionary drive to insure the success of the entire hive during swarming.

One review of research reports the specialization of *super-sisters* (also called *patrilines*) in a wide range of bee behaviors—pollen gathering, nectar gathering, entrance guarding; undertaking dead bees, nectar foraging, nest site scouting, queen rearing, oophagy (egg cannibalization), oviposition and larval care in queenless colonies, grooming behavior, plant choice for pollen collection, and foraging distance[26]. The authors then used microsatellite DNA analysis (a system that uses short "snippets" of DNA to identify genetic information) to show that there were 16 sub-families in one colony of honey bees, and that two subgroups were represented in significantly higher levels in two tasks: water collection and scenting. This suggests a genetic component to task choice.

One subfamily of bees with the same father may provide specialized services within the colony. This reflects another advantage of the queen mating to multiple drones and the resulting drone diversity. No one subfamily is apparently able to control a particular hive behavior, but certainly influences the hive's welfare through decentralized decision making.

Because there is no central control of the bee social structure, no governmental center, decisions must be based on group decisions utilizing the different sub-families. We observe colonies make decisions about foraging, nest maintenance, comb building, and reproduction. Perhaps the strongest example of the group decision-making process is in the process of producing a new queen, which we will discuss next. We will follow that with a discussion on how colonies make decisions about the comb building process.

A. Queen rearing decision-making

Queen replacement occurs in the hive during the whole colony's instinctive reproductive division, the process we call swarming. Queen replacement also takes place when the queen fails to produce the normal amount of worker brood, in what we call the supersedure process, or when the queen is accidentally killed or lost, using the emergency response. Researchers[27] have reviewed the literature and divided the queen replacement process into three discrete behaviors: queen production (selection and feeding), queen emergence, and surplus queen elimination. There are also differences seen in individual queens, such as in piping behavior, when an audible 'piping' sound made by one queen serves to delay the emergence of other mature queens from their queen cells. The queens doing the "piping" have been shown to have the highest rate of becoming the new queens in their hive.

---

[26]Per Kryger, Ute Kryger & Robin F. A. Moritz. 2000. Genotypical Variability for the Tasks of Water Collecting and Scenting in a Honey Bee Colony. *Ethology* 106: 769-779

[27]Tarpy, D.R., and D.C. Gilley. 2004. Group decision making during queen production in colonies of highly eusocial bees. *Apidologie* 35: 207-216

Queen rearing decisions

Honey bees rear surprisingly few queens during the replacement process, perhaps as few as 3-6, and rarely more than 24 individuals, starting many and finishing few. This is in sharp contrast with the 5,000 to 20,000 drones produced by the average colony during one season. Swarming behavior is observed only when conditions favor the collection of pollen and nectar needed to support high brood rearing and queen cell production. New queens are started in queen cups prepared for the queen to lay into; they are on a queen track from before the egg is laid, unlike emergency queens. Sometimes the workers place royal jelly in queen cups before the queen lays into them. In fact, a queen larva receives continuous and abundant royal jelly from large numbers of nurse bee visits. Christine Peng (University of California, Davis) estimated that 200 nurse bees are able to make enough royal jelly for one queen cell. The chemical content of the royal jelly constantly changes as the larvae develop. About 24 hours before the queen larvae pupate they are provided a great amount of the rich food, before the cell is sealed with wax by the worker bees.

The total time for queen cell construction, egg laying, larval hatching and feeding is 15 to 16 days (less in African bees), depending upon genetic and environmental differences. The different subfamilies may attempt to eliminate larvae that might become queen. If a frame of newly hatched larvae is placed into a recently de-queened and artificially broodless colony, a large number of cells will be started as emergency queen cells, perhaps as many as 200 on one frame. But as larval feeding progresses the number of queen cells dwindles. Part of this may be due to less than ideal conditions for cell development, for queen cells are very sensitive to chilling and overheating and may be rejected if they are on the perimeter of the comb where the temperature is less than optimal. Worker bees may decide to destroy a queen cell at any point during its development. In queen rearing operations, the number of cells the day after the they are sealed is larger than the number ready to emerge. Some of this cell count reduction may be a form of hygienic behavior removing diseased individuals, and some may be due to the decision making process of the bees.

There is adequate evidence to show differential treatment of certain eggs, larvae and pupae destined to become queens over those that fail to become queens. During the incubation period, worker bees vibrate certain cells. The workers "shake" queen cells for 1-2 seconds at approximately 16 Hz. Some cells are shaken three times as much as others, although this does not predict outcome. Instead, queen cells that are started earlier are found to be shaken more, and have higher emergence success.

In emergency queen cell production, the age of the brood used for cell production determines the fate of the queen cell; full developed queen cells will be destroyed if they contain the wrong age brood. Thus the queen is able to monitor the developing queen and eliminate those queens that will not become vigorous queens.

Efforts to prove that super-sisters, with a level of relatedness of 0.75 (on a scale of 0.0 to 1.0), favor queens from their subfamily over half-sister queens, with a degree of relatedness of 0.25, have failed to show that there is a clear and statistical significant bias. But if workers do not select super-sisters for queens, they clearly employ group decision making in an effort to improve the quality of the queen produced in the hive.

Emergence of new queens

Worker bees routinely keep fully developed queens imprisoned in their queen cells for prolonged periods of time. I witnessed a dramatic example of this when I inspected a Russian colony during peak swarm season (all colonies in the apiary had swarm cells after a very rainy buildup period, not just the Russian colonies). As the colony owner and I opened the hive we observed many queen cells. I suggested we harvest a few cells and use them to make up increase colonies, so we carefully cut a few cells off the comb and momentarily placed them on top of the neighboring hive. As we inspected the remaining frames in the colony we noticed virgin queens running about on the combs, and soon I was rapidly stuffing queens into empty cages I carried in my bee suit pocket. By then the queens from the cells we placed on the hive cover were emerging. The simple act of opening the hive disrupted the worker bees ability to confined the queens and prevent them from emerging.

After our momentary excitement died down I looked at the queen cells and saw that some queens had cut open the cells to emerge, but the workers had imprisoned them by adding additional wax to the slit at the tip of the cell where the queen had cut open the pupal silk and wax. It was through this narrow slit where the worker bees feed the queen inside the cell-prison. While F. Huber first recorded this process in 1792, it is still a dramatic and exciting experience to observe. Our timing was unique in that we observed a large number of queen cells, over a dozen, of mixed ages and some with confined queens.

Why do bees keep perfectly good queens entombed in the cells? There is some evidence that the worker bees are using their collective consensus building to control the fate of these queens. The imprisoned cells that are shaken by worker bees are more likely to be the first to emerge. The workers control the timing of queen emergence by adding or reducing wax deposits on the incision at the tip of the cell (they must keep just ahead of the queen, for our hive visit must have disrupted the bees ability to control emergence). Finally, it is possible that bees selectively confine half-sister queens over super-sister queens, one of the best proposals yet of potential genetic control of the final queen.

Queen elimination

Once a queen emerges from a cell, the worker bees continue to control her fate. They can favor one queen so she emerges first, allowing her to systematically sting her sisters still confined in their queen cells. Or the workers may kill the queen by arranging two queens to "duel" on the comb until one queen is dead (This is the simplistic example of queen elimination seen in nature films). The workers often have control over the success of the fight, keeping one queen in a "ball" of bees so she is less able to defend herself, indeed, a queen is more likely to win if related to the worker bees.

New queens usually do not leave with the primary swarm (the colony's original queen does this), but will depart with an after-swarm—this is most often the explanation for the workers keeping queens confined in their cells. Many swarms contain multiple virgin queens. This may reflect the large number of confined virgins, as well as a selective advantage of getting a new queen to the new nest successfully. Once the hive is in the new location, dead virgin queens may be found at the entrance of the hive, so the queen to queen duel happened in the new nest site. The exact mechanism of preferential treatment of one queen over another is unknown, and requires further study.

Selection Pressure

Control of the selection, release and destruction of queens is one of the most critical duties the worker bees have, if not the MOST important in terms of colony survival and selective advantage. While a colony could employ a policy of "any queen will do" the selection pressure on a colony appears to produce a significant number of queen candidates that are evaluated at several points in the production cycle and culled to eliminate those queens that are poorly produced, developmentally defective, wrong-aged, or of unacceptable genetics. The ability of a colony to survive within an environment places strong selective pressure on queens that must perform within this environment, and the only means for elimination is through the worker bees.

B. Colony decision-making and worker and drone comb construction

During the active foraging season honey bee colonies are forced to decide between the need for food for the colony *or* the need to build open comb for storage of incoming pollen and nectar. Either the colony builds comb for food storage (a process they cannot reverse once the comb is built), or they may utilize food coming into the hive and, because of the lack of empty comb, run the risk of loosing abundant food when it becomes available. Recently Stephen Pratt[28] reviewed colony control aspects of worker and drone comb construction. He reported that in nature a new colony builds 1 m^2 of comb in one year, or a little more than ten ft^2. A colony metabolizes about one-eighth of the honey it collects during the year to secrete wax for comb construction. Bees must respond to hive and environmental conditions in such a manner as to optimize comb construction while preventing over- or under-production of wax comb at the cost of lost resources.

Lacking a central government, the worker bees must have some feed-back mechanism to reach a consensus of *when* it is beneficial to build comb, and in the case of worker and drone comb production knowing which *type* of comb to produce. Pratt has determined that to build comb colonies must fill two needs: "adequate nectar collection in the field, and the filling of their comb above a threshold level." The combination of *comb fullness* and *nectar intake*

[28] S.C. Pratt, 2004. Collective control of the timing and type of comb construction by honey bees (*Apis mellifera*). *Apidologie* 35: 193-205

must align to stimulate worker bees in the hive to secrete wax and initiate comb construction.

The concept of comb fullness may remind the reader of G.M. Doolittle's recommendation to keep three full frames of honey full in the colony all of the time (See Doolittle, *A Year in an Out-Apiary*, 2005, and Connor, *Increase Essentials*, 2006), suggesting that a certain level of fullness of the comb is required for bees to build new comb and initiate other expansive behaviors. Without a certain level of comb fullness, the colony will not build comb. Once the amount of filled comb and the incoming level of food reached the critical threshold, both comb construction and food storage will proceed.

We see this in the buildup period of the spring when the bees are actively gathering pollen and nectar, but are not engaged in new wax building. Even if supers filled with foundation are added to the hive, the bees often delayed building new wax in these frames. During this time, if you look at the brood nest of the colony, you will find that the bees are busy filling the brood rearing areas of the hive with food reserves—pollen and nectar essential for new bee production and colony growth. The bees may be stimulated to draw out a brood comb if a frame is removed and a frame of foundation is added to the center of the brood nest. But sometimes this frame serves to divide the brood nest, as the bees are not yet ready to draw wax and build comb.

Seasonal patterns of nectar availability show that surplus nectar is gathered only on certain days, just 14-35% of the days in the nectar season. When bees are not gathering nectar it is because the flow has curtailed, perhaps because one plant has stopped blooming and the bees are awaiting the next plant to flower. The comb production of a hive reflects this pattern, and since there are generally several major periods of nectar availability during the season, there are corresponding periods of active comb building. When the supply of incoming nectar stops, the bees stop comb building as well; the bees have adapted their comb building to suit several periods of rich food availability during the season.

The individual bee plays an important role in this process, since returning foragers must find house bees to unload their nectar. The house bees are also involved in wax secretion, so there is a feedback mechanism at work that allows the bees to monitor incoming food and wax secretion. Then, when the supply of nectar falls, the stimulus is absent and the house bees stop producing wax.

The actual wax-building process is highly dynamic, as one bee adds wax to a cell, another bee moves to the same area and reworks the same area of comb. This process continues until the comb is built, filled and capped. This lets all the bees know the cell size being produced (worker or drone), and ensures uniform cell construction.

Drone or worker comb?

Small colonies of bees are unlikely to produce drone comb unless the queen's status supports the production of drones. Queenless colonies are more likely to produce drone and large-celled worker comb, but if queen pheromone is provided, the bees produce only worker cells. In hopelessly queenless colonies with laying workers, continued drone brood production is the only genetic legacy the colony is able to pass on to the pool of reproductive bees.

In normal colonies, there is an average of 17% drone comb. Since the bees do not produce 17% drone brood, we must remember that this comb is used for both male bee production and for food storage. When colonies do not have drone comb present in their hive, they will instinctively build drone comb in and effort to balance the ratio of the two comb sizes. When there is a large amount of drone comb present, the bees automatically adjust and build more worker comb.

How do the bees know how to do this? Since the bees make direct contact with the combs, they must somehow measure the number and ratio of drone cells and worker cells. Since house bees place their heads into cells routinely, they may measure cell size in the same manner that the queen does, and this may provide them with the stimulus to produce the necessary cell size. Thus a large amount of drone comb, and even drone brood, has a strong inhibitory effect on production of more drone comb. The bees are doing nothing more than measuring the hive environment, and adjust it to some inherited, genetically regulated standard.

Finally, there must be some sort of comb building peer pressure—preventing one worker bee from building one drone cell in the middle of a comb of worker cells. The individual bees are undoubtedly influenced by the collaborative method of same-cell size construction on the comb, and this keeps the comb construction uniform and highly efficient. When damaged comb is placed in a hive the bees will sometimes build drone comb in the area where worker comb once existed. It is not the nature of the damaged comb that determines the type of cell that will be built there, but the integrated dynamic of the comb building bees, their evaluation of the colony's comb needs, and the ratio of comb that already exists within the hive that makes their comb building decision.

Honey bee genome

The honey bee was the fourth insect to have its entire genome sequenced resulting in 11,000 coding sequences. This compares to 13,500 sequences in the fruit fly and 14,000 in the mosquito. Initial analysis by geneticists reveals that the honey bees evolved in Africa and migrated to Europe at least twice. Isolated for long periods of time, various races of honey bees developed with their own unique genome pattern. A Western Europe subspecies was introduced into North America in 1623, followed by an Italian subspecies introduced in the late 1800s. Most recently an African subspecies was introduced into South America in the 1950s and has moved through South America and into North America, including the lower states of the United States.

Compared to other insects, honey bees do not have as many genetic sequences that protect them from disease. There are fewer gene sequences that produce detoxifying enzymes that break down insecticides, partially explaining why honey bees are so sensitive to chemicals, as well as why colonies rely more heavily on behavioral mechanisms of disease resistance like hygienic behavior and polyandry.

Breeding schemes for honey bees

Line Breeding—Any beekeeper who uses his or her best colonies as the basis of the next generation of queens and drones is employing the technique of *line breeding*. A majority of line breeding beekeepers use just one or two criteria in their selection process, usually those colonies producing a large brood nest and a large crop of honey (These two characteristics are statistically correlated and are also correlated to the amount of pollen a colony collects). Line breeding beekeepers may select for a number of additive characteristics that help them decide which breeder queens to use to produce the next generation of queens and drones.

Line breeders must use a number of queens for their selection pool, grafting from as many queens as possible that exhibit the desirable characteristics. If they do not, there can be a narrowing of the diversity of characteristics, resulting in a *loss of vigor* due to inbreeding. This is different from the inbreeding effect that results when the alleles for sex determination pair up to reduce the percentage of brood viability. The loss of vigor and sex-allele inbreeding may appear together or in isolation. Vigor loss is common in inbred-hybrid programs and contributes to the high management cost of keeping inbred queens alive.

The best way to counteract a loss of vigor is to maintain a diverse drone population of unrelated drones in the mating area, as outlined by David Tarpy and Tom Seeley above in this section. Constantly introduce unrelated bee stocks with the characteristics you desire and produce drone from them. Even small scale beekeepers are able to influence resulting colony vigor by introducing new and unrelated drone lines into their mating area.

Crossing lines (Hybrid bee formation)— G.H. "Bud" Cale, Jr., in his doctorate on the inbred-hybrid system, demonstrated that by creating inbred lines and crossing them, creates hybrid bees that usually exceeded the parents lines performance due to the effect of *hybrid vigor, or heterosis*. He used this concept to develop several hybrid bees: the Starline, Midnite, Cale 876, Cale 235 and the Hi Queen (for high alfalfa pollen collection). The first two hybrids were open mated in areas of saturation with drones furnished to complete the cross. The other hybrids were the product of instrumental insemination and were available only during the 1970s.

Certain queen producers produced the so-called "double hybrid" which mated Starline virgins to Midnite drones.

The method Cale used to generate grafting mothers for honey producers and queen propagators was called the "criss-cross" method. In one year virgin queens were raised from the H line, and instrumentally inseminated to G line drones. These breeder queens were shipped to cooperators (who were under contract to pay a royalty for every queen sold or used in their operation) and daughter queens were in turn mated in areas saturated with drones raised by queens produced the *previous* year. These were drones raised in colonies headed by queens grafted from breeders made from aE virgins instrumentally inseminated to F drones.

The second year the breeders switched. The breeders were sent aExF grafting mothers to mate to the HxG drones now in the colonies. So in the first year the worker bees that were being produced were HGxaEF, and in the second year the worker bees were aEFxHG. Cale admitted to some "maternal effects" switching the cross, but considered them minor in comparison with the elegance the criss cross program provided for the production of tens of thousands of genetically identical queens and colonies each year. For the record, the H and G lines were predominately Italian in origin, the aE line was developed as part of the high-alfalfa collection program, and the F line was from a Carniolan queen found in California during the 1940s. It had been out-crossed to select for yellow color, and by 1976 had been out-crossed to Italian stock at least twice, and then re-selected in an effort to maintain the vigor of the stock and to add a third sex allele to the line.

The F line was also used as the drone side in the instrumentally inseminated Cale 876 hybrid, and gave me countless challenges in my years with the program. The line reflected its Carniolan origin by cutting back on egg laying whenever the flow was over, a characteristic Bud Cale wanted in the hybrid because it balanced the broodiness and pollen-focused from the other lines in the cross. Interestingly, like the Russian bees, this line was hard to introduce into unrelated colonies in the pure form (even a F queen mated to unrelated drones). As a result we only introduced F line queens into colonies that already contained the F line in their pedigree. We produced more F line drone mothers than any other line to meet the huge demand for F drones.

This sort of unique management added to the annual cost of maintaining inbred lines. With about a dozen inbred lines to maintain, we invested an estimated annual labor cost of 200 to 400 hours *per line* for maintenance and instrumental queen maintenance (because of lost vigor and sex allele problems found in inbred lines). As popular as the hybrid bees were, the extremely high labor costs are one reason they are no longer available. The other reason was quite simple: they possessed no unique tolerance or resistance to tracheal or varroa mites. The Starline bee had been the predominate type kept at the University of Minnesota when Dr. Marla Spivak and Gary Reuter started to develop the Minnesota Hygienic bee.

Many queen producers have crossed *races of bees*, notably Brother Adam during the on-going development of the Buckfast bee. By examining various crosses, Adam selected queens for use to establish the Buckfast line. Adam seemed to employ a combination of hybrid crosses and line breeding to establish and maintain the Buckfast. I do not know how the line is currently being maintained in North America.

Closed population breeding—The New World Carniolian bees are developed through a process of selection called a *Closed Population Breeding program*. One reference to learn more about his process is Laidlaw and Page's *Honey Queen Rearing and Bee Breeding*. The authors state the purpose of a closed population breeding program is to maintain "as many sex alleles as possible in the breeding population." This method reduces the loss of alleles that result in missing brood or "shot brood." Page and Laidlaw's plan required the maintenance of 35 queens with a predicted freedom from inbreeding of 10 to 20 years.

To develop the New World Carniolan, Sue Coby and Tim Lawrence collected queens from the United States and Canada that were believed to be descended from Carniolan stock. They were tested to determine if they produced characteristics of Carniolan bees, and became part of a group of 35-50 queens that produced both virgin queens and drones. In each generation, five to ten virgin queens were mated with pooled and mechanically mixed semen from a number of drones. This meant that each queen was mated with semen collected from the gene pool of the population.

When breeders use pooled semen from the drones, the differences seen in the colonies were due to the queens, not the drones. From the colonies produced, 35-50 queens were selected to replace the previous generation of queens. Each queen candidate was evaluated in a pre-screening program that included brood viability, temperament (defensive behavior), spring buildup (worker population), cleaning behavior (removal of debris from the hive), occurrence of disease, swarming (presence of swarms cells), and color (black). Colonies that were not eliminated from the pre-screening evaluation were then evaluated for honey production.

The closed population breeding plan's major advantage (over inbred-hybrid schemes) is that it starts with a larger number of initial colonies and provides *uniform diversity of drones* present in the spermatheca of each queen. The resulting colonies have a wide diversity of subfamilies that will potentially produce a superior colony. Finally, the costs of maintaining 35 instrumentally inseminated colonies is smaller than the huge costs of maintaining 12 inbred lines. Because the closed population system does not require or want inbred lines, the cost of maintaining 35 to 50 colonies is much, much less, even though many queens must be inseminated and tested to become the final number in the scheme.

In Canada, Tibor Szabo developed a method of evaluating short-term (ten-day) weight gains as a predictive tool for honey production, and added this to a program there. Those queens with the highest weight gain in 10 days were included in the pool of 35-50 breeder queens.

Laidlaw and Page state that the closed population breeding program produces better queens than the hybrid-inbred system because "the best stock possible is no better than the best possible in the original population."

Since 1982, when Page and Laidlaw published the closed population breeding scheme, other breeding programs have been developed with combined aspects of the closed population system and traditional line breeding techniques. Unfortunately, few of these programs benefit the work-a-day beekeeper. One hope I have in writing this book is to stimulate more beekeepers to develop their own versions of a closed population of bees that are evaluated for productivity, gentleness, mite tolerance, and wintering ability. Drawn from local stocks, a number of similar programs could develop in different parts of North America, serving the beekeepers in each of the regions. I also hope to see active selection of bees using this technique in areas of African bees as a method of providing competitive yet acceptable colonies for beekeepers of all sized operations.

Instrumental insemination of honey bee queens

Mature honey bee drones may be stimulated by physical contact and pressure to ejaculate. The fully inverted drone endophallus has tan semen floating on a bed of white mucus. With experience, an inseminator is able to collect the semen and not the mucus with a hollow syringe like device. A virgin queen, usually about seven days after emergence is opened and a set amount of seminal fluid inserted into the virgin's median oviduct. A flap of tissue must be moved out of the way to accomplish this act.

Since the virgin is not allowed to fly, she requires one or two exposures to carbon dioxide before and during insemination. This stimulates the hormone that causes eggs to develop.

One single drone produces about 5 million sperm. A healthy queen will have between 5 and 8 million sperm in her spermatheca. As part of the multiple mating behavior of virgins, up to 85 million sperm may be temporarily housed in the median and lateral oviducts after natural mating. With instrumental insemination, a "full" amount of semen is considered to be 8 microliters of semen. This is inserted all at once when a single insemination is used. A few inseminate with two smaller batches of semen one to three days apart to increase sperm migration into the spermatheca.

Inseminators must maintain a clean work area, and add an antibiotic in a 0.9% saline solution to protect bee tissues and prevent disease infections leading to queen death.

Single drone inseminations are often used in research projects to eliminate the variability provided by multiple mating. Some researchers use queens grafted from the same breeder mother and drones produced by the same queen. Various clever and innovative techniques have been developed to maximize the power of instrumental insemination.

Queens that have been instrumentally inseminated should be kept in a nucleus, the entrance blocked with queen excluder, or caged in a queen bank, for four weeks prior to introduction into a regular colony. Perhaps because instrumentally inseminated queens are watched more carefully, the reports of introduction failure and early supersedure are not unusual. Unfortunately, this may only reflect the low rate of introduction and early supersedure experienced by *all* queens that are produced by humans, naturally mated or instrumentally inseminated. Further work needs to be done on the physiology of queens in queen banks and the exact mechanisms at work in the development of mated queens.

It is possible to harvest semen from a queen and use the semen to mate with her daughters. Self fertilization (autogamy) of queen bees using instrumental insemination leads to these values of inbreeding coefficients (F): ½, ¾, 7/8, 15/16, 31/32.

Drone sperm is easily stored at room temperature for several weeks, even months. Capillary tubes are filled with semen and sealed at both ends with petroleum jelly to prevent contamination and dehydration. Antibiotics must be in the saline solution to reduce bacterial growth. Shipment of drone semen from one laboratory has been done to provide semen for insemination of breeder queens.

Long term sperm storage has been investigated by Drs. John Harbo and Anita Collins. The successful storage of semen is a notable goal for stock preservation programs, and is overdue in light of the loss of breeder queens due to mite die-off. At present, at least 50% or better viable sperm preserved semen can be used to inseminate queens and will provide enough time for a breeder to rear daughter queens and obtain traits for incorporation into a breeding program.

Instrumental insemination and local breeding programs

I do not think it is necessary for every beekeeper who wants to breed bees to become proficient in instrumental insemination. While a useful skill, it is one that is not often used, and the insemination device, microscope and carbon dioxide equipment cost many thousands of dollars. I recommend that groups of beekeepers interested in breeding find and financially support one or two area inseminators for the production of their breeder queens. They should be individuals with a clearly scientific orientation to beekeeping. Virgin queens and drones may be mailed or hand delivered to the laboratory, inseminated, and held for a month before being returned to the breeder. While I have inseminated many thousands of queens, I prefer to have someone else do the work, some one who has equipment familiar to them and polished skills. A package of caged virgins and mature drones (and adequate numbers of nurse bees) can even be express shipped to the insemination service.

Apparent equal sperm utilization

Most research shows that sperm is released randomly from the spermatheca. There have been a few reports of clumping of sperm and uneven offspring. I am not convinced either way. Perhaps both happen under different conditions.

Resistance to brood diseases and mites

In the 1950s Dr. Walter Rothenbuhler published work showing that two genes are responsible for hygienic behavior of removing diseased brood from a sealed cell. One gene allowed the bees to uncap the cell, and a second gene allowed the bees to remove the cell. Uncappers did not clean out cells that were already open, and Cleaners did not uncap sealed cells. Thus, both genes are required for this to work. Plus, both genes are recessive, and must be present in both the queen and drone side of the worker bees for expression of this behavior.

In 1993 Marla Spivak and Gary Reuter started to test colonies at the University of Minnesota (based primarily on Starline colonies), using liquid nitrogen to kill a circle of brood. They counted the dead brood removal in 24 hours, and wanted to see at least ninty-five percent removed for the stock to enter their breeding program. Since the colonies were already productive bees, they maintained colony gentleness and productivity. These colonies are the basis of the Minnesota Hygienic Bees (HYG)

At this same time period a number of scientists worked to find survivor stocks in apiaries that had successfully made it through an attack of *Varroa destructor*, the varroa mite. These queens were collected by Dr. John Harbo at the Baton Rouge Honey-Bee Laboratory and were selected solely for their ability to withstand varroa mite attacks. Harbo observed that these bees had a low level of varroa mite reproduction, and they called the SMR bees, for Suppressed Mite Reproduction.

When Abdullah Ibrahim and Marla Spivak examined the mechanisms of resistance of these two lines to *Varroa destructor*, the SMR colonies removed more of the mite-infested pupae than the HYG colonies. They wrote *Our findings indicated that bees bred for SMR express hygienic behavior; adult bees selectively remove pupae infested with mites. In addition, there is an effect of SMR pupae that reduces mite reproductive success that requires further investigation.*

The result of this research is that the SMR bees are now called Varroa Sensitive Hygienic (VSH) bees, representing another form of hygienic behavior within the colony than found in the Minnesota Hygienic stock (HYG).

There is growing use of hygienic bees to combat varroa mites as part of an effort to use Integrated Pest Management (IPM) techniques and reduce dependence on chemical treatment of bee colonies. Hygienic stocks are often used in combination with screened bottom boards and powered sugar dusting. To use the Minnesota Hygienic bees in a beekeeping operation, Dr. Spivak recommends that the bees be at least 50% hygienic in order to get successful mite (and disease) control. To achieve this concentration of apparently recessive traits means that over 50% of all the drones a HYG virgin mates with carry the hygienic genes. As we learn more about the similarities and differences between HYG and VSH bees as well as other mite-resistant stocks, we may well be able to develop mating schemes that allow us to provide a diversity of drones that all carry essential hygienic characteristics that will produce an optimum of colony diversity and strength.

Queen with a problem laying eggs. After a worker vibrated the abdomen of the queen with her legs, the queen produced 3 or 4 eggs outside the cell. A partial blockage of the oviducts with mucus might explain this behavior. This queen survived over a year, but the colony remained extremely small.

V. A model plan

Over the past few years I have had discussions with many beekeepers and it is clear that a vast majority of them are actively seeking independence from the inconsistencies of queen propagators living hundreds or thousands of miles away. Their problems include difficulty obtaining live, on time delivery, low queen introduction success and low longevity of queens in the hive as seen in early supersedure. Finally, if successfully introduced, the performance of these queens is less than desired—many have little measurable tolerance against varroa mites.

These same beekeepers argue they cannot conduct their current beekeeping activities and raise quality queens too. Good luck to the large commercial honey producers who decide that they will master queen rearing in one season. For a long time I have recommended that all beekeepers learn queen rearing in order to understand the biology of the process and the difficulty of raising queens well. It's a fact that many commercial honey producers raise all or most of the queens they need in their operation and frequently the owner runs the queen mating yard—it is that critical to the success of the entire beekeeping operation.

This section proposes a drastic change in the way we raise queens and use them in the United States and Canada. In this plan we will seek local, improved stock, and local production sites within a comfortable day's drive. Most of these queens will be raised in the late spring and summer, when many commercial queen propagators are stacking up their nucleus boxes for the season. They may overwinter summer increase colonies with new queens, as discussed in *Increase Essentials*.

The solution is local

Not every beekeeper wants to raise queens. We must find and support financially motivated and well trained beekeepers who are willing to raise queens for the local market. If we purchase one hundred $20 queens and half are lost, and have done so year after year, it seems we might be better off paying $40 each for 50 queens that have much higher acceptance, performance, and mite tolerance. They should be non-defensive and productive.

Within every state or provincial bee organization there are beekeepers with the skills, interest, training and overall abilities to raise queens of quality. Look at the Ontario bee breeders, who straddle the 43rd parallel as does my Michigan home, and their success producing queens. Ontario beekeepers were forced to produce their own queens when bees were no longer allowed to cross the US-Canadian border. Ontario queens are not ready until late spring or summer. They are not ready for April 1 packages. This is a key change—we must use a new calendar for queen production and when we start new colonies.

So let's draw some borders and keep out stock that is from the southern states, western states, areas with African bees, hive beetles and beekeepers with old trucks. And foreign countries with unknown parasites and diseases. Seriously, let's think local. Find a half dozen interested beekeepers in your area who are willing to produce queens. Place an order for 25 queens for the next season and see what happens.

We have few models for large-scale queen production in northern locations. So we should look at mid-sized queen production, although there are relatively few of these in northern areas. However, I feel that if the money comes, they will grow in size.

Sideline queen producers

There are thousands of sideline beekeepers in this country working another job, or are retired, or do something that keeps them from expanding beyond 100 to 300 colonies of bees. If you are one of these beekeepers, you need to consider raising queens for local sale. Maybe you have sold queens when you had extra queens from your own queen rearing activity.

What will it take you to produce 500 queens next year? It sounds like a lot, but if you can sell 500 queens at $20-30 each, you have serious cash coming in from your beekeeping that wasn't there before. In this system you are NOT going to raise queens during the early spring but will wait until swarming season to raise queens and continue until August or September.

Pull out a calendar and mark ten consecutive weeks from late May to August when you have ten weeks. This is your season. Ten weeks producing 50 queens each week.

If you are near the 40-45 degrees latitude you may start raising queens after fruit tree pollination ends in mid May. The colonies will be strong and ready to swarm or be part of your queen rearing/nucleus operation. You can produce queens up until the first of August, delivering the queens as you travel to EAS meeting that year in early August. All of your mating nucs have ripe cells installed in them, the mating nucs are on a summer flow. If all goes well you will winter these nucleus hives and sell them with new queens next season.

How many mating nucs do you need?

Plan to keep queens in their mating nuclei for three weeks, giving them time to more fully develop. If you do that you will need a *minimum* of 150 mating nuclei. Take inventory of the equipment you have in storage. If you divide double deep or medium honey supers in half to make up mating boxes, you want at least 75 divided boxes plus some for spare. During the winter you can divide the colonies with plywood or some other thin wood product, and give each half of the box an entrance opposite the other side. A quarter inch plywood bottom can be cut and nailed to the bottom. Use plastic feed bags or silt fencing for an inner cover, and a cover.

The mating nuclei need to be ready when you can pull out 150 or more frames of brood and bees after fruit bloom is over. This timing correlates with the peak swarming season, so you are probably saving some colonies the chore of swarming by taking out frames of brood and the bees on them.

Forget about baby nucs, half frame nucs and their cousins. Use full frame nucs so you do not need to invest in new equipment. If someone gives you brand new odd-sized equipment, assembled and painted, consider their offer. But ask why they picked you.

Year one

During your first year you will not raise any queens for sale, but will perfect your queen rearing skills by producing queens for yourself. You will select colonies that will become future grafting mothers and drone mothers (or drone mother breeders). If you have local colonies that has survived varroa mite attacks under your climatic conditions, you should include them in your program. Obtain as many local colonies that have good production, locally-adapted characteristics, and some ability to withstand mites.

Russian bees—Over 100 years ago Carniolian bees were taken to Eastern Russia and exposed to varroa mite populations from the Eastern honey bee. The survivor stock that was collected by USDA researchers, led by Tom Rinderer, is much different than the mostly-Italian stock found in North America. Some beekeepers love these bees, others hate them. Most agree they are very different in buildup behavior. In the model plan, Russian strain can be incorporated into the breeding plan to introduce varroa mite resistance without relying entirely on just one stock. USDA/Baton Rouge

Next, you should buy or trade one or more of the proven hygienic stocks and incorporate them into your operation. Look at stocks of Minnesota Hygienic, University of Georgia, Purdue University, New World Carniolian, VSH (SMR) and USDA Russian, as well as queens from key beekeeper-breeders like Joe Latshaw, Dann Purvis, Kirk Webster, Mike Palmer and others who have been selecting stocks for several years. Find out what retired USDA scientist John Harbo (who developed the VSH (SMR) stock) is doing as a private bee breeder.

Finally, put your ears up and listen for any local beekeeper who *claims* to have survivor stock, or colonies that have not required mite treatments for 4 or more years. Attempt to get that stock, or at least graft daughters from it (purchase a frame of brood with suitable aged larvae and graft queens at home).

Get as many of these stocks into your operation as possible, with a minimum of SIX unrelated groups (assume each queen is heterozygous, so 6 times 2 yields 12, about the number of drones mating with each queen). These become your potential pool of target drone producers. This will address some of the issues raised by Seeley and Tarpy about the benefit of increased drone diversity.

Do not use stock from Australia, large queen propagators or others who have placed emphasis on filling boxes of bees rather than quality of the queens. Locate commercial breeders who sell instrumental inseminated queens of improved stock, (such as Tom Glenn, Sue Cobey and Joe Latshaw), who may provide you with high quality, instrumentally inseminated breeder queens. This is the fastest way to obtain traits like hygienic behavior.

In the first season you will want to get these queens installed or grafted so you can get some of these bees under observation. Take as many notes as you need. Once your queens are established and her bees have repopulated the hive, ask a hot-shot beekeeper or professor of apiculture to go through the bees with you. Ask to pick her brain. You may or may not want to follow her suggestions but compensate her for time and expenses.

Develop a short list of *measurable characteristics* in your bees—number of stings, pounds of honey, wintering survival and absence of disease. Remove any colony that has foulbrood or chalkbrood, and pinch the queens of any colonies that darn your socks with stingers every time you walk into the yard. It is awfully hard to get rid of traits like that, so don't start with them!

Using your list of characteristics and the hard data you have collected, assign a score or ranking for each trait. Develop your own point system, and add up the scores and pick out the top colonies. Finish the data collection in the fall and do the math over the winter. Keep the evaluation as simple as possible!

Year two

Selecting breeder queens and drone mothers

At the beginning of the second year, evaluate the top 20 percent of all colonies that survived the winter by using the liquid nitrogen test to kill a circle of brood. Count the dead brood removed in 24 hours. Ultimately you want to obtain 95% or more brood removal. Since you already ranked these queens on non-disease criteria, you are safe making these observations for hygienic stock. Bees lines selected for just one trait do not usually do well as general producers.

So, it is spring of the second year and your inventory of hives might look like this:

10	Minnesota hygienic queens
10	Local queens grafted from a survivor hive
5	Queens purchased at a beekeepers auction
10	Queens purchased from instrumental insemination service (naturally mated)
15	VSH x hygienic daughters from II breeder
15	Colonies from your original operation

Now you make your final evaluation and test for hygienic characteristics. Here are the results.

Minnesota hygienic queens. You have good first impressions of this stock, and marked two queen for grafting and the rest for drone production

Local queens grafted from a survivor hive. One of these will be a grafting mother, and 4 will be useful as drone producers. The rest had bad chalkbrood and the queens were pinched.

Queens purchased at a beekeeping auction. None of these showed any hygienic behavior, but they were gentle and productive, so they will produce drones.

Queens purchased from California instrumental insemination service. These queens were grafted from II daughters. One will be a possible grafting mother, and three will produce drones. The others were eliminated for various reasons.

Double mating nucleus hives in California. While this system produces a large number of quality queens, it may not be suitable for the plan in this section.

VSH x hygienic daughters from II breeder. This was a pretty impressive group except 4 queens did not lay a big pattern and were pinched. Three queens are scheduled as grafting mothers.

Colonies from your original operation. A few colonies showed a little hygienic behavior, but not a lot. One was found with American foulbrood (the bees were killed and the equipment moved out), and another was removed for chalkbrood. Four more were removed because they stung too much—the queens accidentally ran into your hive tool . The rest will be used as drone mothers. In summary you have—

Stock	Breeders	Drone Mothers
Minnesota	2	8
Local survivor	1	4
Auction	0	5
California	1	3
VSH x hygienic	3	13
Original	3	9
TOTAL	**10**	**42**

This California mating uses special frames and special boxes. This plan in this section uses standard hive frames and hive bodies to simplify the operation.

Following this scheme you have eliminated the lower 25% of your colonies from being part of the breeding program. Since they were all colonies that you once thought had something to contribute, you have made some significant selection. You were also trying to come up with a critical number of colonies to use as drone mothers, and managing 42 drone mothers could mean you will have a minimum of (42 x 1600 =) 67,200 drones in the air to mate with your queens at any time. Each virgin queen will have 1344 *target* drones to select from in the mating arena and to compete with non target drones you cannot avoid. If you are a good drone manager, you may have two or three times that number of drones (134,400 to 201,600).

Mating nuclei

Colonies you do not use for queens or drones will provide brood and bees when you make up your mating nuclei. You may start making up mating nuclei a few days before the queen cells are ripe and ready to be installed. But don't start too soon or the bees will start queen cells—if so, cut them out, or you may have a "side-comb virgin" that will mess up your plans. It's crazy to make work for yourself.

Once the queen cells are in place, watch to make sure the nuclei maintain strength in both bees and brood, since smaller colonies can fail for many reasons. Swap positions if one is strong and another is weak. Add a frame of brood if one becomes weak. If there is not a flow underway, feed the colonies a 1:1 sugar water solution.

Wait at least 21 days (instead of the traditional 14) to harvest a mated queen. She will have had full frames to lay into, and if you made up the nucleus with lots of bees and brood there will be a large population of workers. By letting the queen expand the nest size, you also increase her pheromone production and "maturity" as a queen. After a cycle or two of queens you may need to remove some of the brood to keep the unit small.

Hold the queens in the nucleus as long as you can. If one beekeeper cannot pick up his order, call another from your backup list of queen customers to keep on schedule. Pull the queens in the afternoon and if the beekeeper can't pick them up that evening, meet them the next morning at a central location to make delivery.

Your objective is to have these queens installed the same day they are removed from the mating unit, or the nest day. This will help increase acceptance levels and provide a superior queen.

You may want to offer a service and load up the mating nucs and take them to a local beekeeper/customer's hives and add the queen and a frame or two of brood. Requeen using a nucleus works with little disruption in the queens egg laying. You should charge a huge premium for this sort of service—think about your last computer repair bill when you set your fees.

The mating area

In this book we have covered the flight behavior of queens and drones, and the elaborate means they seem to go to prevent inbreeding. As a result, you should start with a mating area of 1 mile radius and place drone mothers or drone holding colonies in locations 0.5 to 1.0 miles from your mating yard. I suggest you use a township map or a map off the internet to help you select locations for these colonies. Use members of your local bee club to help you locate these hives. They may hives in some of these locations, so ask to place queen excluders on these hives to prevent their drones from flying. Offer to requeen any colony that looses a queen during this time period.

If your queen business takes off, you will want to expand your radius to 2 miles, and perhaps to 3 miles. That is about 30 square-miles, and a great deal of real estate in which to control mating.

Mating accuracy

I know of no simple way to evaluate mating accuracy in this size operation. Larger operations can use genetic markers, but your stock is new and in constant change. The bees should be variable in color and other characteristics. You must simply evaluate each queen as you pull her from the nucleus and ask yourself—*would I want this queen in one of my colonies?* Your customers should be reminded that you are engaged in a new breeding program, and their feedback is part of your learning process.

Overwintering nucleus hives

If you have 100 good queens in strong nucleus hives, prepare them for winter using one of the methods described in *Increase Essentials.* When you make your first spring inspections provide protein food to insure colony survival. At the end of March or early

April inspect each colony and help them build up. Within a month they should be strong and ready to move into a customer's empty bee hive. Don't be in a huge hurry to get nucleus colonies to the beekeeper, since they will be far ahead of any package colony, and by waiting you can watch them carefully. If you have done your work correctly these colonies should be ready for a super in late May or early June.

Costs and benefits

It costs both time and money to establish a localized, survivor stock program. In many areas there is a perception that you should discount these queens. In fact, these are premium queens, home-grown, and worth a premium fee. Higher costs will drive some beekeepers away, but eventually, when your customers talk about their success and performance of the queens, even the most bargain-oriented beekeeper will be interested in "trying a few" at your asking price.

Index

Printed in China